Beginner Series:

Drums Method

LEVEL I

Ray Rojo

Violet Anamnesis Publications

San Diego, California

Violet Anamnesis Publications
15658 Bernardo Terrace Suite B
San Diego, California /92128

Beginner Series: Drums Method Level 1 / Ray Rojo —1st Ed.
ISBN 978-1-944213-05-3

Table of Contents

CHAPTER

1

Getting to Know the Drum Set

Welcome to Level 1 of this series of books that will guide you through a journey of learning and understanding how to play the drum set. The very first step to learning how to play an instrument is to familiarize yourself with it. Therefore, it is important that we know all of the components of and the different instruments that form a drum set. The following picture portrays a standard drum set with the names of all the individual instruments:

All of these separate instruments serve an individual purpose and all of them put together make a drum set. As said before, this is a very standard drum set, but there can be many different configurations of drum sets. A common change to this configuration is having fewer pieces; for example, fewer toms. It is very popular to only have "tom 1" and the "floor tom" on the kit, with no "tom 2". The opposite is also possible and we can add more pieces to the drum set. It is very popular to have more than one "crash cymbal" as part of the kit. Make sure you familiarize yourself with all the names in the picture so when they come up again in the text you will know to what it is we are referring.

The Theory Behind it All

In order to successfully use this book, or any of the books in this series, we have to first familiarize ourselves with a few concepts. This chapter will explore and explain many of these concepts and it's important that we understand them before we can move on.

Pulse or Beat

A pulse is very often referred to as the regular and steady beating of the heart, an even and steady beat that keeps us all alive. In music, the pulse is what makes us tap our feet and bob our heads to songs. Just like with our hearts, it is even and steady and keeps the music alive. Now that we have a reference to the word pulse, think of each pulse as the strongest accent in time during a song or piece of music.

Rhythm

Rhythm is everything for drummers. It refers to patterns of accented and unaccented notes, which may have different values (we will define and get into note values later in this book), inside a specific pulse. As we move forward in this book and the series, we will also learn many different kinds of subdivisions of time, different rhythms, and how to put all of it together.

The Importance of Counting Out Loud, Reading, and Writing Music

As musicians, reading music is just as important as playing it. Understanding music on paper gives us a visual reference to what we play and enhances the understanding of the mechanics behind it. Another benefit is that being able to put our musical ideas on paper and reading someone else's without having to listen to any music expands our range of musical possibilities immensely. By being able to count while we read/play, we strengthen the visual/mechanical reference between what we see and what we play. In my personal experience, reading and transcribing are also some of the most entertaining things to practice.

Tempo

Earlier, we talked about pulse (or beat). Tempo refers to how fast or slow that pulse is going to be. We measure time in hours, minutes, and seconds. In music, we measure tempo in relation to how many beats we have in one minute. This is called "beats per minute" and is represented by the initials "bpm".

The Staff

When writing notes in a regular notebook, we follow lines to make sure that the size of our writing is correct and that we are writing in a straight line. In a similar manner, when writing music we follow these five lines called the "staff":

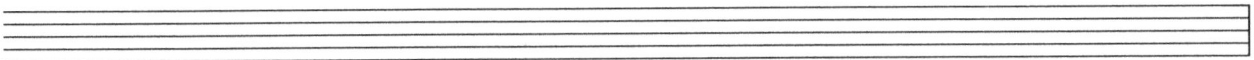

When writing music on a staff, each one of the lines and spaces represents a specific note. In the case of drums, each of the lines represents a specific drum or cymbal. The meaning of what each line represents can change depending on the clef that is drawn at the beginning of the staff.

The Clefs

In music there are many different clefs. The treble clef, the bass clef, the alto clef, and the rhythm clef (or drum clef) are some of the most commonly used. Clefs are always written at the beginning of the staff to indicate what instrument or range is written. For the purpose of reading drums, we are only going to be concerned about the rhythm clef:

Drum Notation

Now that we know about the staff and the "drum clef", it is time to give each space and line a specific meaning. This is going to be our "drum key":

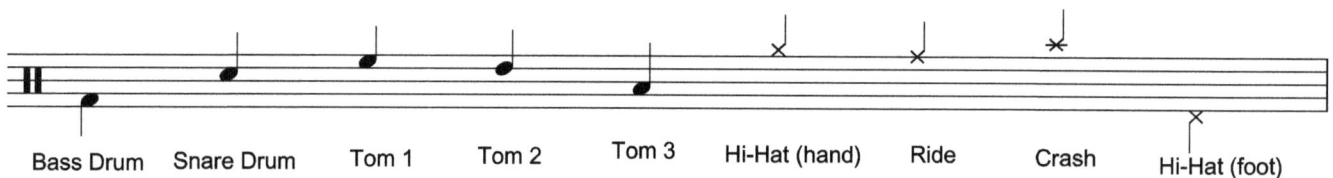

| Bass Drum | Snare Drum | Tom 1 | Tom 2 | Tom 3 | Hi-Hat (hand) | Ride | Crash | Hi-Hat (foot) |

It is important to note that this notation is not completely universal. Different books may have different drum keys. For the purpose of this series we will always use this notation. It is also important to note that the hi-hat and other cymbals are written with an "x", this helps to separate the drums from the cymbals making it easier for us to read it.

Bar or Measure

A bar or a measure in music refers to everything that fits within two bar lines. Depending on the time signature, the number and the value of the notes that are inside of a bar may vary. Here's what two empty bars look like. Note that they are separated by a "bar line":

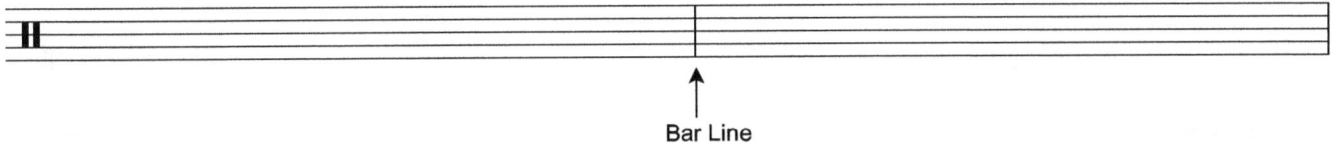

Bar Line

Time Signatures

A time signature is the fraction that we use to specify how long each bar is and on which note value we are going to focus. To be more specific, let's use an example: a time signature of 4/4 tells us that there are four quarter notes in one bar. How do we get to that conclusion? The numerator specifies how many beats are in each bar and the denominator specifies which note value gets one beat. Following that rule, there are going to be 4 (because of the numerator) quarter notes (because of the denominator) in one bar. If we have a time signature of 5/8, it means we have five eighth notes in one bar. Here's what the time signature looks like at the beginning of the staff:

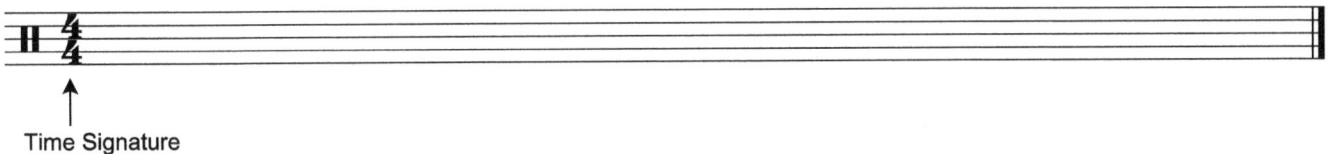

Time Signature

Repeat Sign

The repeat sign is used to indicate that one measure (or several measures) is to be played twice. However many measures are between the start repeat sign and the end repeat sign are to be played twice:

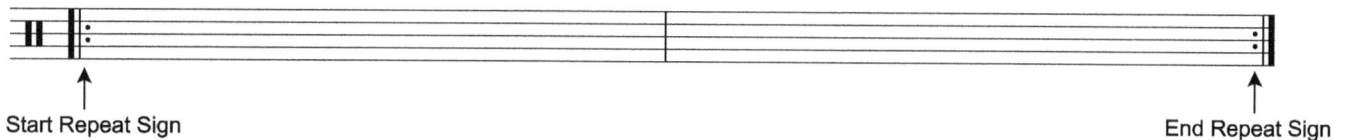

Start Repeat Sign   End Repeat Sign

If the repeat sign wants you to go back to the beginning of the chart (or the beginning of the example), oftentimes the start repeat sign is not written:

End Repeat Sign

CHAPTER

Basic Technique and Proper Posture

To play a drum set, we can use several different "tools". The most common and the focus for this level will be drumsticks. As we learn more and move forward in this series we will get into the use of brushes and hot rods as well. This next picture shows a pair of sticks on top of a snare drum

Drum Sticks

Choosing the right pair of sticks for you is very important. Some of the factors we need to consider are the weight, the length, and the width of the sticks. All of them will affect your playing and it is important that you play with sticks that feel right in your hands. You don't want to use a pair of sticks that require you to use extra energy because they're too big, or feel like you are playing with toothpicks because they are too small. I encourage you to try different brands and models until you find something that feels comfortable.

Introduction to Hand Technique, Single surface

There are two ways to hold the drumsticks. One is called "traditional grip" and the other is called "match grip". Inside of the match grip technique there are several variations: the German grip, the French grip, and the American grip.

First, let's take a look at match grip. As the name implies, match grip refers to holding one of the sticks with one hand and matching that grip with the other hand. This way both hands work in the exact same way. The first step is to establish the main grip point and in this case, it will be between our thumb and index fingers:

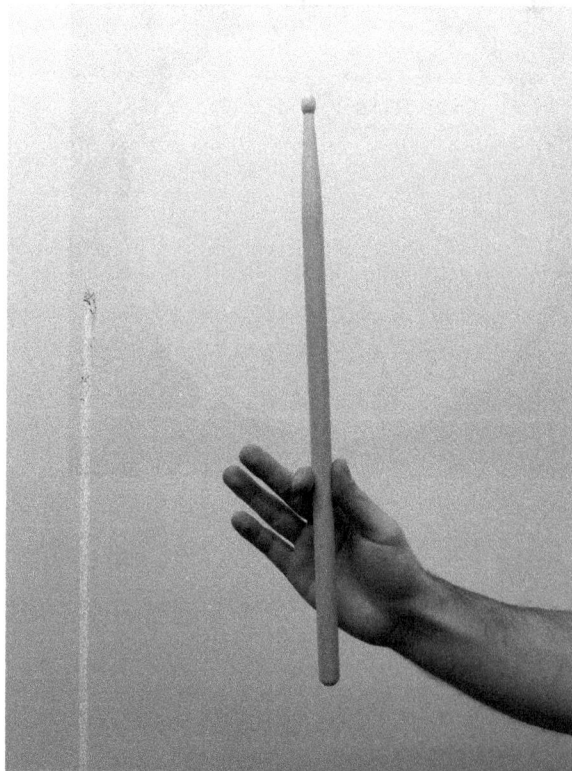

The next step is to wrap the rest of our fingers around the stick:

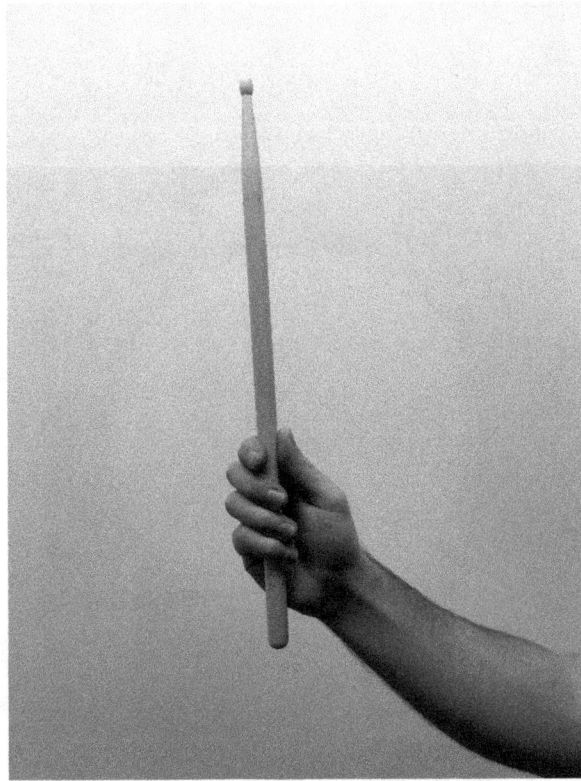

Because this is match grip, both hands will follow the same process to hold the sticks regardless of being right-handed or left-handed. Now that we have established the main grip point we are going to move on to the three different possibilities of match grip. All the examples will be shown over a snare drum (single surface) to have a clearer image of what they are supposed to look like when we practice technique.

The first possibility of match grip that we are going to talk about is called "German grip". In order to execute this grip correctly we need to position our hands with palms facing the ground and our thumbs facing each other. When using this grip there should be an approximate angle of 90 degrees between your sticks:

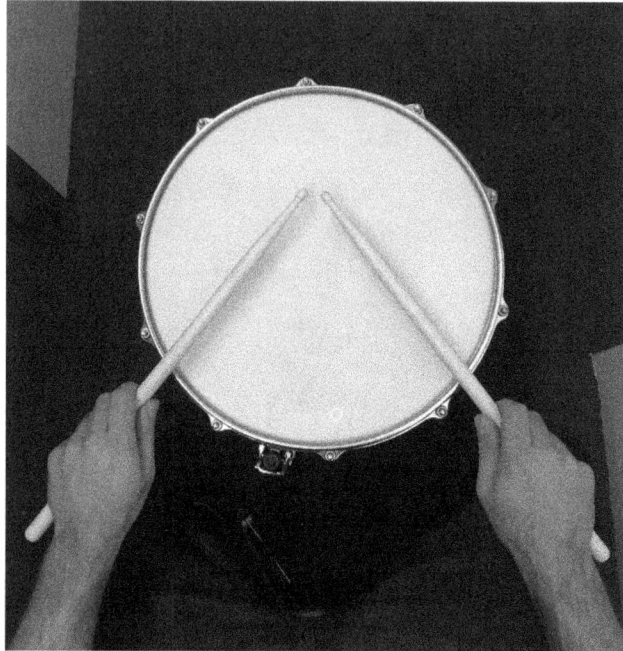

The next possibility is called "French grip". In order to execute this grip correctly our thumbs need to be facing up and all other fingers will be facing each other. When using this grip the sticks should be completely parallel to each other:

The last possibility of match grip is called "American grip". I think of this grip as the middle point between German and French grip. If German grip is palms flat to the ground, and French grip is 90 degrees from that, American grip would be 45 degrees:

Second, let's take a look at traditional grip. This technique of holding the sticks originated when drummers used to march with a snare drum whose strap would wrap around only one of their shoulders. This caused the snare to tilt and forced drummers to hold the sticks this way to effectively hit it with both hands. For right-handed drummers, the hand that holds the stick with traditional grip is the left.

The main grip point for traditional grip is here, resting on your hand between your thumb and index finger:

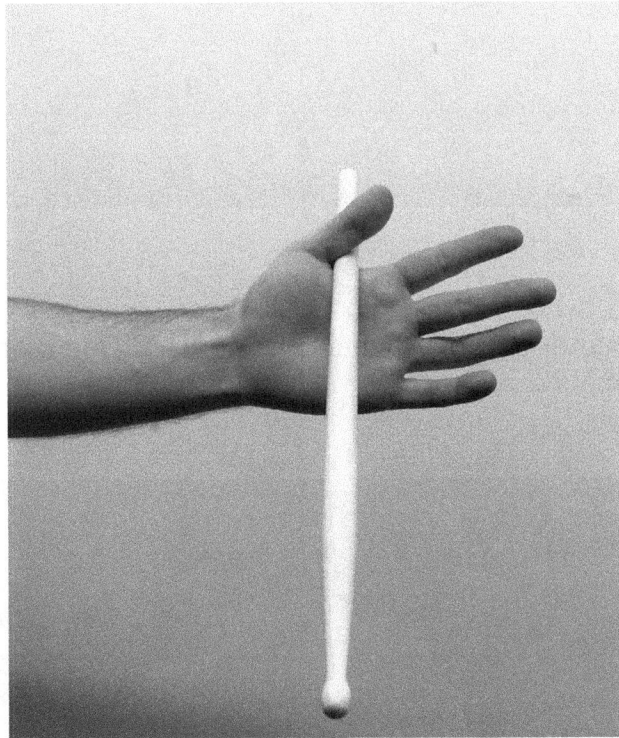

Once the main grip point is established we hold the stick between our ring finger and our middle finger:

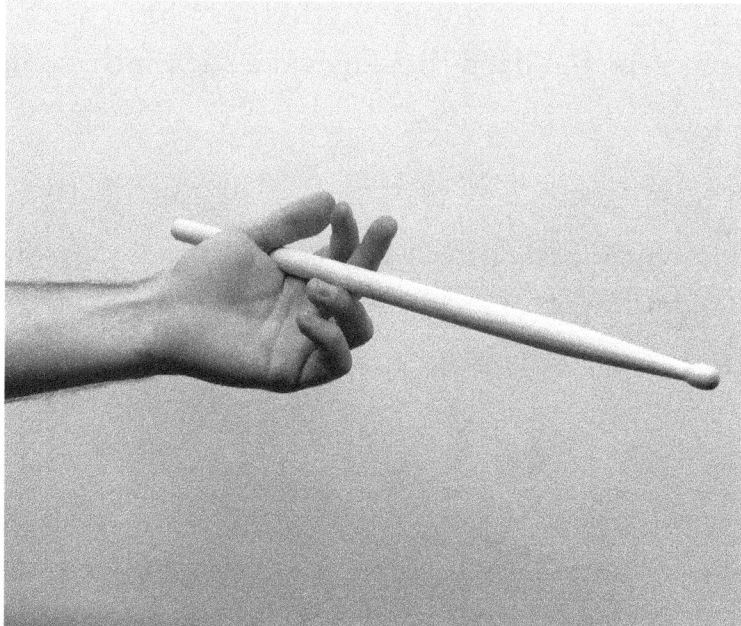

Here's what both hands look like when playing traditional grip:

All of these techniques are very common and used worldwide by drummers of all styles. It is important to note that technique is very much like choosing a pair of drumsticks; you have to use what feels more natural and comfortable for you.

I personally prefer to play using match grip, switching between American and German grip, because they feel more natural and have proven to be the most effective in my personal development. I encourage you to try and focus on these two grips, but not to neglect trying all the other techniques since they might suit your playing better.

Proper Posture behind the Drum Set

Now that we've talked about how to hold the sticks, it's time to focus on how to sit behind the drum set. Like hand technique, there are a few different things to consider:

- Use a good drum throne or drum chair. This provides good support for your back which helps you remain relaxed and avoid possible back injuries caused by sitting tensely while practicing.
- Seat height. Comfortable seat height improves balance, which helps to relax your lower back and causes less stress on your legs when you play.
- *Be relaxed!* Relaxed playing is possibly the most important thing that we've talked about regarding technique and posture. Always be relaxed and avoid tension anywhere in your body while you play or practice. Pay attention to your breathing and try not to tense up or run out of air.

Let's analyze the height of the drum chair. I find that it's better to have your drum chair high enough so that your thighs are just a little bit higher than if they were parallel to the ground:

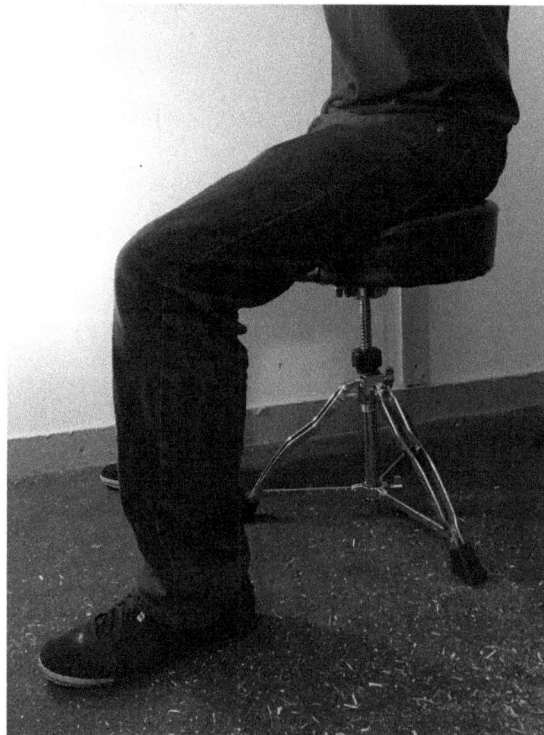

This allows us to play with a lot of power because we can still use the weight of our legs, yet its high enough for us to not have to carry the entire weight of our legs before we strike the drums.

Try to avoid sitting like this, much lower than the first example picture:

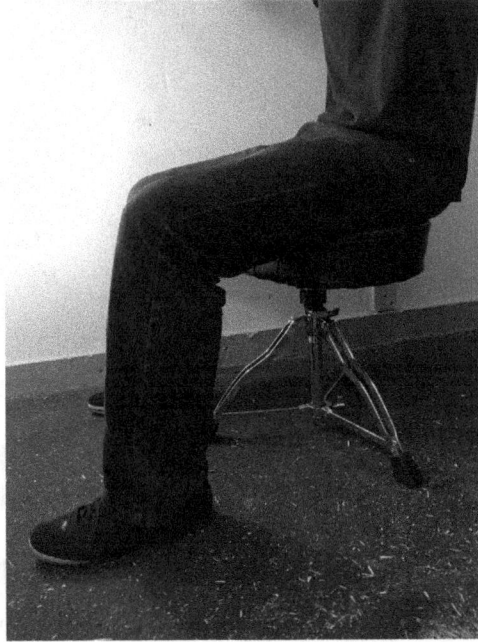

Sitting this low still allows you to use the weight of your legs, but it creates more tension in your lower back by forcing you to carry the entire weight of your legs before each stroke.

You also don't want to sit like this, much higher than the first example picture:

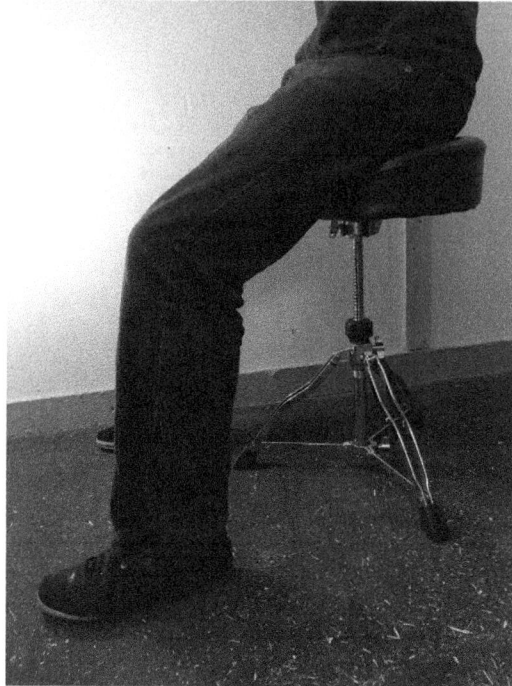

This helps you to not have to carry your legs at all and won't cause extra stress on your lower back, but by having your legs so high you lose the possibility of using their weight to get more power from your strokes.

As a conclusion to seat height, remember that by keeping your legs at a little over the 90-degree angle from the floor you find a happy medium where you don't have to carry your legs to use your feet, and at the same time you don't lose power. Just like with hand technique, I encourage you to try sitting very low, very high, and everything in between to find what's more comfortable for you. After all, what is more comfortable for me may not work well for you and vice versa.

Foot Technique

There are also a couple of different ways we can play the pedals with our feet. In this book, we will be focusing on two techniques: The "heel down" technique and the "heel up" technique. Please consider the previous section on seat height when trying to find the technique that is more comfortable for you.

Let's take a look at heel down technique first. It is executed by holding your heel down on the ground at all times and pushing the pedal down with the ball of your foot. This technique works better for quiet playing because by anchoring your heels to the ground you isolate the shin muscles and take away the weight of your legs in your strokes. By taking the weight away, you lose a lot of power in the strokes.

Now let's look at heel up. It is executed by having your heels slightly off the ground at all times and then pushing the pedal down with the ball of your foot. This technique allows you to use more weight from your legs, which results in much more powerful strokes. Think of the motion of your ankles as if you were trying to bounce a basketball with your feet. You want to make sure you are using your ankles to move your feet up and down.

Try to avoid lifting your heels up too much. This leads to unnecessary tension in your legs:

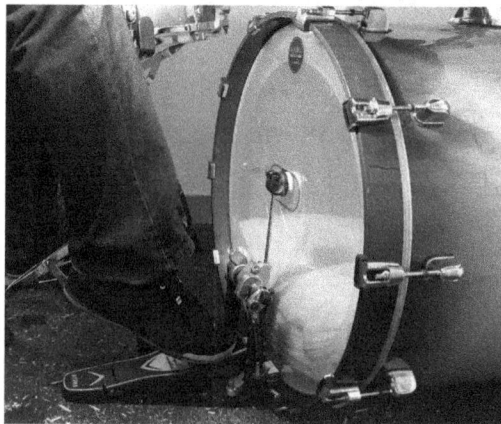

Hand Technique behind the Kit

After talking about many kinds of grips and showing an example of how they look on a single surface, we need to move it to the drum set. It is important to observe that it's all right to not hold a rigid "German grip", or any other particular grips, when we are sitting behind the kit. The motions of moving around the kit and playing surfaces that are at different heights and positions can cause this to happen. This is not a bad thing as long as it feels natural, you are aware of what you are doing, and you stay relaxed at all times.

Here are examples of things to be aware of regarding hand position behind the drum set. Start by sitting comfortably at a good height while holding a pair of sticks and let your arms hang completely relaxed next to your body. Remember to keep a straight back.

Then, move your hands up to the drum set. Keep your shoulders relaxed and your elbows close to your body, just like they were when they were hanging:

You can also play the hi-hat with your left hand. This method of playing is known as "open handed" playing:

Avoid creating tension in your shoulders by moving them up:

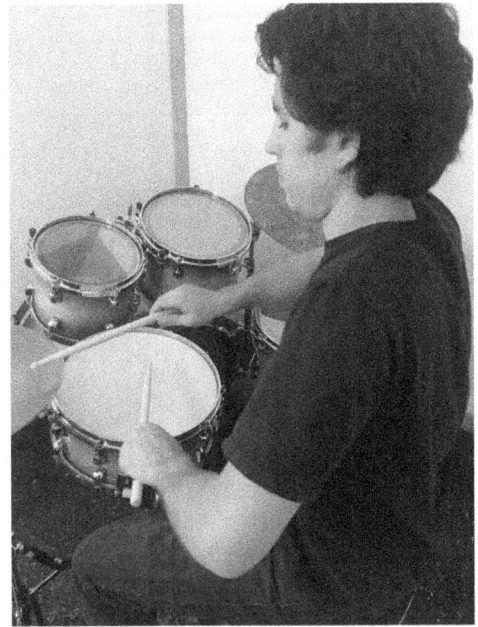

And avoid separating your elbows too much from your body.

CHAPTER

3

Your First Time Reading, Your First Time Grooving

In the previous two chapters we've reviewed the parts of the drum set and where and how we write them. Now it is time to take all of that theory and put it into practice. Before we do that, there's one last step: introducing our first note value and our first counting system.

The Quarter Note

The quarter note is the foundation of our first grooves, our first reading examples, and it is the first note value that we learn how to count. This is what a measure of 4/4 looks like when it is full of quarter notes:

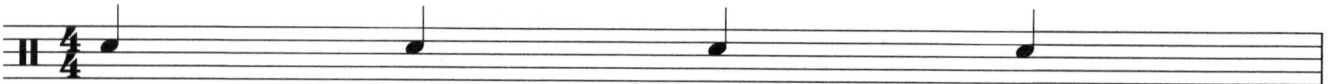

Please note that, as talked about in chapter two, we are using the "drum clef" (or "rhythm clef") and the time signature states that there are four beats in a bar, and that each quarter note gets one beat. The place in time where the quarter notes land is often referred to as the "downbeat".

We are now going to add a counting system to this measure of quarter notes. Because we are in 4/4, we are going to count from 1 all the way up to 4, giving each quarter note a number. Please note, we will not make it to 5. After 4 we will go right back to number 1. Always count this out loud as you play it with your hands or tap your foot. Make sure that you are tapping at the same time you are saying the numbers.

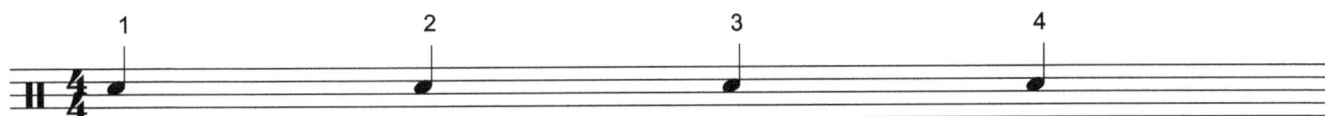

Every note value we learn has an equivalent rest. Rests stand for "silence", meaning we don't play. This is what four quarter note rests look like. Please note that even though it means don't play, we still want to count through the rests to make sure we respect their full value.

Reading Example 1

Now that we understand the quarter note and its equivalent value as a rest, here are a few reading examples to practice our counting and reading.

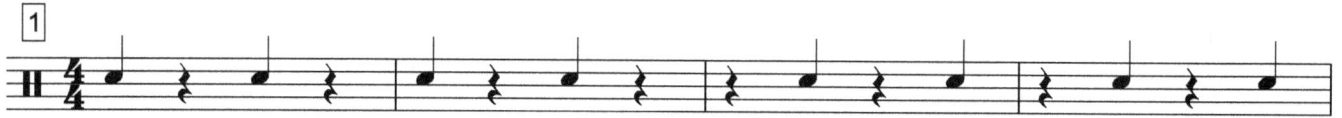

The Challenge of Coordination

The most difficult (and yet most fun!) part about drumming is, without a doubt, the coordination. Drumming requires us to play with all four limbs at the same time, but often every limb plays something different. Sometimes two or more limbs play at the same time and sometimes they never do. In this first level we focus on using only three limbs. We are going to leave the 4th limb (which will be the left foot) out of the equation, but be prepared for its introduction in the later levels of this series!

Your First Groove

It is time to finally get on the drum set and learn a groove! We are going to use all the theory we've learned in this level so far and put it into practice. We are going to start by playing a quarter note groove that looks like this:

In order to develop the coordination necessary to properly execute this example, we are going to break it down into four steps. Steps 1 to 3 will only use two limbs, and step 4 will be our full groove. Remember to always count out loud while playing all the different steps.

Step 1:

The two limbs that we are using in Step 1 are the hands. Our hi-hat hand will play all the beats (which means it will line up with all of the numbers), and the snare hand will play on beats 2 and 4.

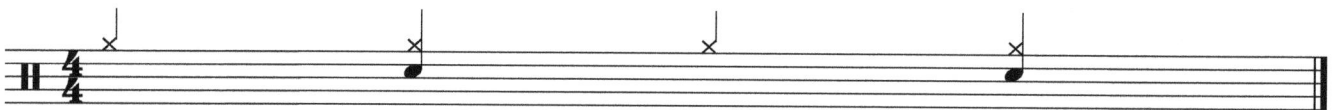

Step 2:

For this step we forget about the snare hand for a moment and instead we add the bass drum on beats 1 and 3. Note that the hi-hat hand is still playing all the beats.

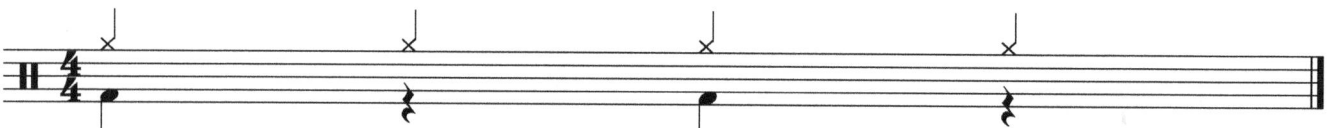

Step 3:

Now, we forget about the hi-hat hand and play only the bass drum and the snare. Just as before, bass drum plays on beats 1 and 3, and snare on 2 and 4.

Step 4:

Now that we have played all of the possibilities with two limbs, it's time to play the entire groove. Remember, hi-hat on all the beats, bass drum on beats 1 and 3, and snare drum on beats 2 and 4.

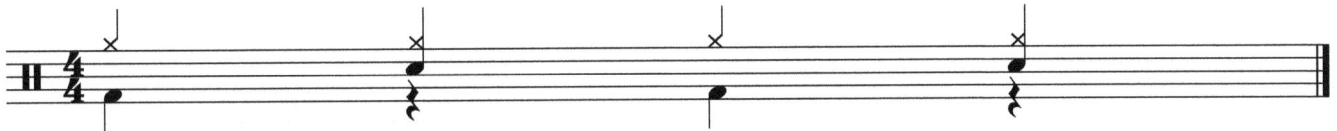

Don't forget to always count out loud.

Variations of Quarter Note Grooves

We have now learned how to play our first groove, and not only that, we learned how to break the groove down to make the learning and coordination process much simpler. This step by step process will not be written down for every exercise (because it would make every level four times the size), however, keep it in mind every time you are facing something new and challenging. Breaking examples down like this will speed up the learning process and make it less frustrating for us as players. Now it's time to play a couple of variations on the first groove:

Half Time Feel

We are now going to slightly change the hand pattern. Our hi-hat hand continues to play quarter notes, but our snare drum hand will now play only on the downbeat of 3. This creates what is often called a "half time feel". It's called that because if we compare grooves with the snare on beat 3 to grooves with the snare on beats 2 and 4, it creates an illusion that we are playing slower or that we are playing in "half time". Here's the simplest version of the half time feel:

We can also have variations to the half time groove by adding/changing the bass drum patterns:

2 Bar Quarter Note Grooves

We have now learned several variations of our first groove and several variations of the half time feel, however; so far each one has been one bar long. In this section we are going to combine the previous variations to form two bar grooves. This gives us many more possibilities for variations. Make sure you focus all the way through. Here are some two bar grooves in both regular time feel and half time feel:

As always, remember to count out loud as you practice all of these examples.

CHAPTER

The Eighth Note

After learning how to count the quarter note and getting comfortable reading quarter note rhythms and grooves, we need to learn how to subdivide the quarter note. In this chapter we are going to learn the 8th note, which results from evenly subdividing the quarter note into two. This means that in the same space where we used to play one note (the quarter note), we will now play two evenly subdivided notes. We want to acknowledge all of the 8th notes when we count as well, so our counting system will change a little. We are going to keep the same numbers as before on the downbeats and add the word "and" for the second 8th note. The second 8th note is often referred to as the "upbeat". This is what a bar of 8th notes in 4/4 looks like:

Just like with the quarter note, the 8th note has an equivalent rest. Each individual 8th note rest stands for half a beat (or half a quarter note). This is what a single 8th note rest looks like:

Reading Example 2

Now that we understand the 8th note and its equivalent value as a rest, here are a few reading examples to practice our counting and reading of 8th notes and 8th note rests. Please note that because the word "and" is long, it is substituted by the "+" sign. This saves us time, ink, and space when we are hand writing our own charts.

9

10

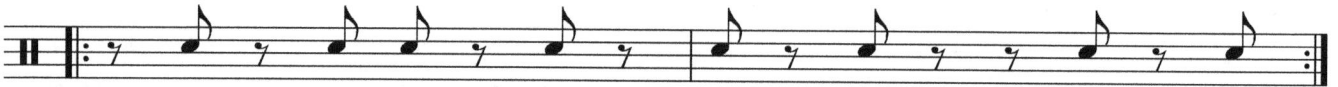

Even though the counting isn't written in all of the previous examples, make sure you practice them all counting out loud.

BEGINNER SERIES | DRUMS METHOD | LEVEL I • 37

Grooving in 8ᵗʰ Notes

We are now going to use the new subdivision we've learned (the 8ᵗʰ note) and put it into practice behind the kit by playing 8ᵗʰ note grooves. By using 8ᵗʰ notes, the possibilities and variations of grooves we can play doubles in relation to the quarter note grooves. This results in a bigger challenge than the quarter note examples we played in chapter 3. Remember to try the 4 step break down and count out loud to speed up the learning process. Here's the first groove we will play using 8ᵗʰ notes. This groove is often referred to as the "2 and 4" groove:

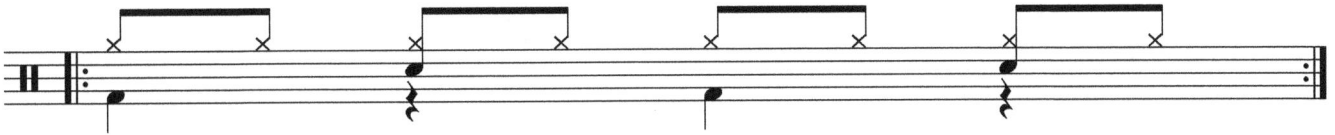

Playing this groove will help us get used to keeping 8ᵗʰ notes with the hi-hat hand and 2 and 4 with the snare hand, something we want to be comfortable with for the next section. When playing the previous example, don't forget to count out loud to strengthen your understanding of what you are playing.

Bass Drum Placement

After playing our first 8th note groove, we will use the same hand pattern to develop strength and control with our bass drum. Here are a few groove examples using 8th notes. Remember that for this section we will always play 8th notes with the hi-hat hand and beats 2 and 4 with the snare hand. The focus of this section should be in the placement of the bass drum:

11

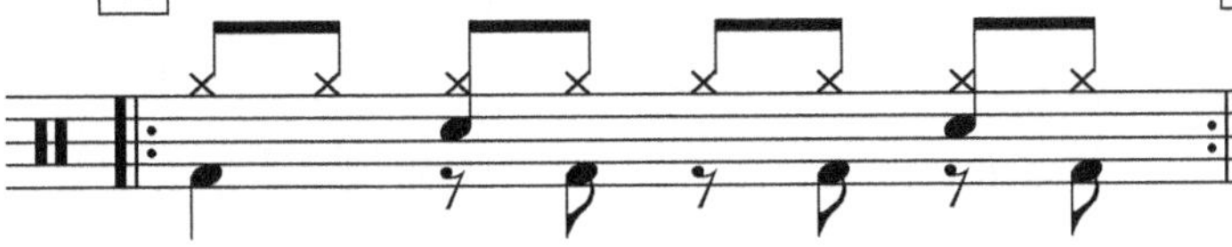

12

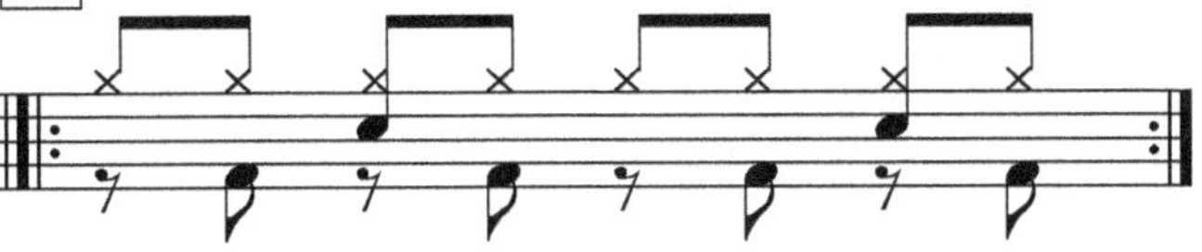

13

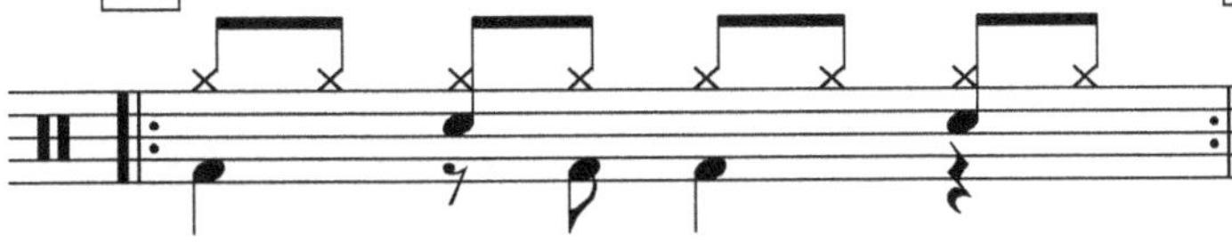

14

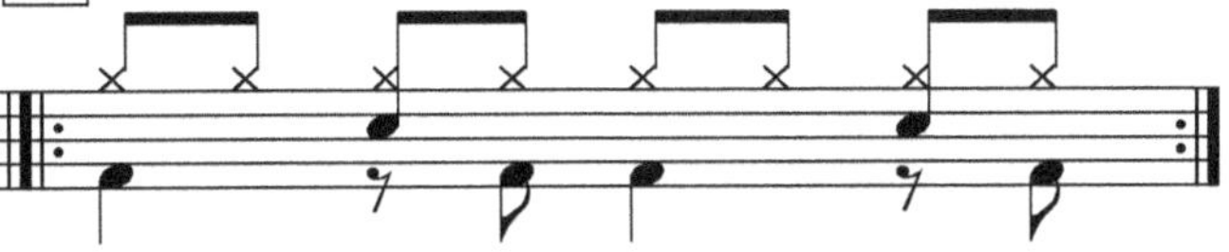

15

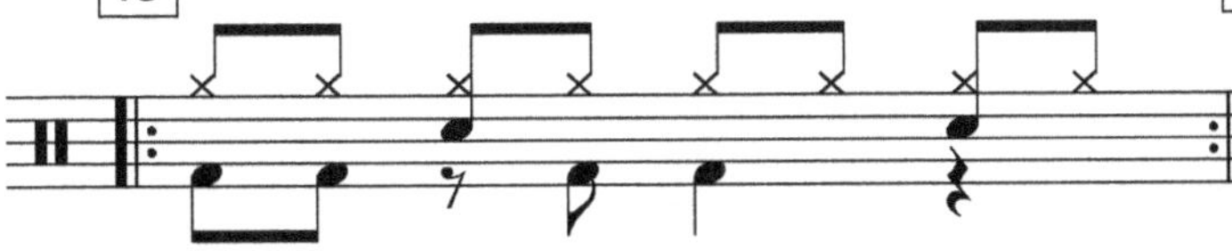

16

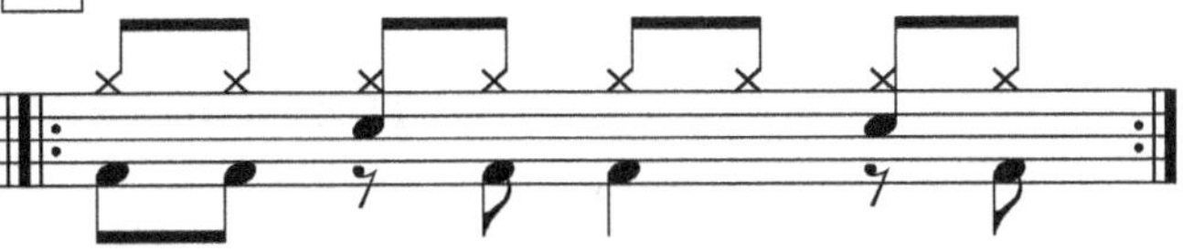

17

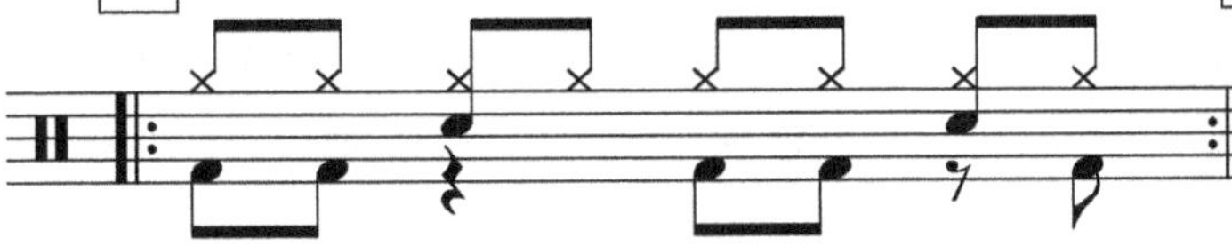

18

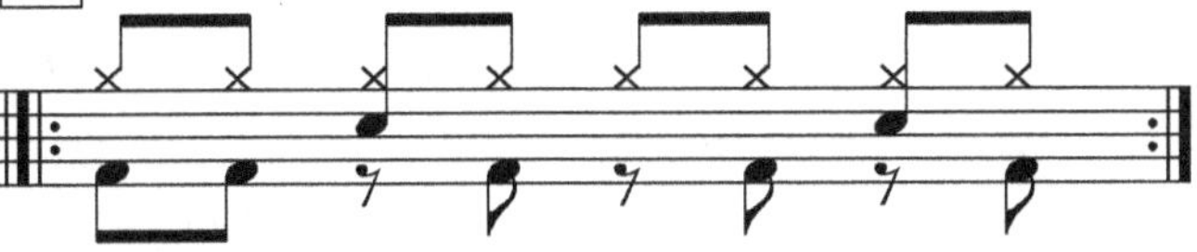

19

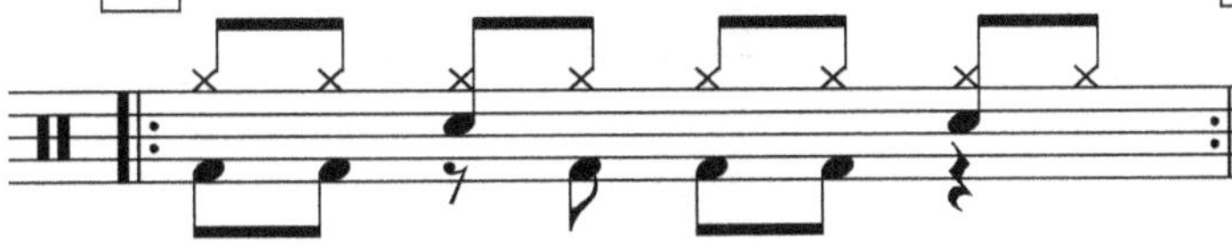

20

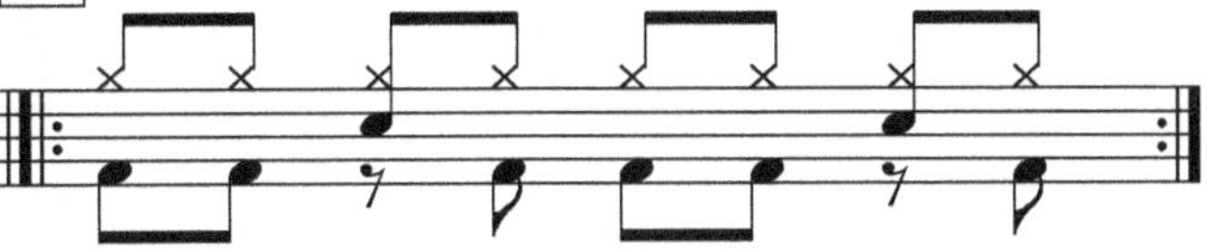

The "Four on the Floor"

Completing the previous examples will help you gain more control over your bass. We will now use that control to change things up a little. Up until this point there has never been a snare drum played in unison (at the same time) with the bass drum. This next example is often referred to as "four on the floor" and has a bass drum on every beat of the measure. This will cause the bass drum and snare to play together on beats 2 and 4. It is very important that we pay attention to the sound to make sure it sounds like one stroke, even though we are hitting two drums. Here's what the "four on the floor" looks like:

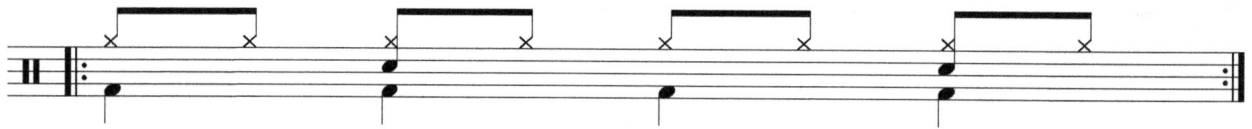

Half Time Feel with Eighth Notes

We have now spent a considerable amount of time working on our bass drum placement and we have learned the half time feel with quarter note grooves. Now we are going to apply the half time feel to our 8th note grooves. Our hi-hat hand will continue to play 8th notes but our snare drum hand will now play only on the downbeat of 3. Here's the simplest version of the 8th note half time feel:

Because we are now playing 8th notes, the amount of variation that we can have is much larger than with the quarter note example. Here are a several variations of the 8th note half time groove:

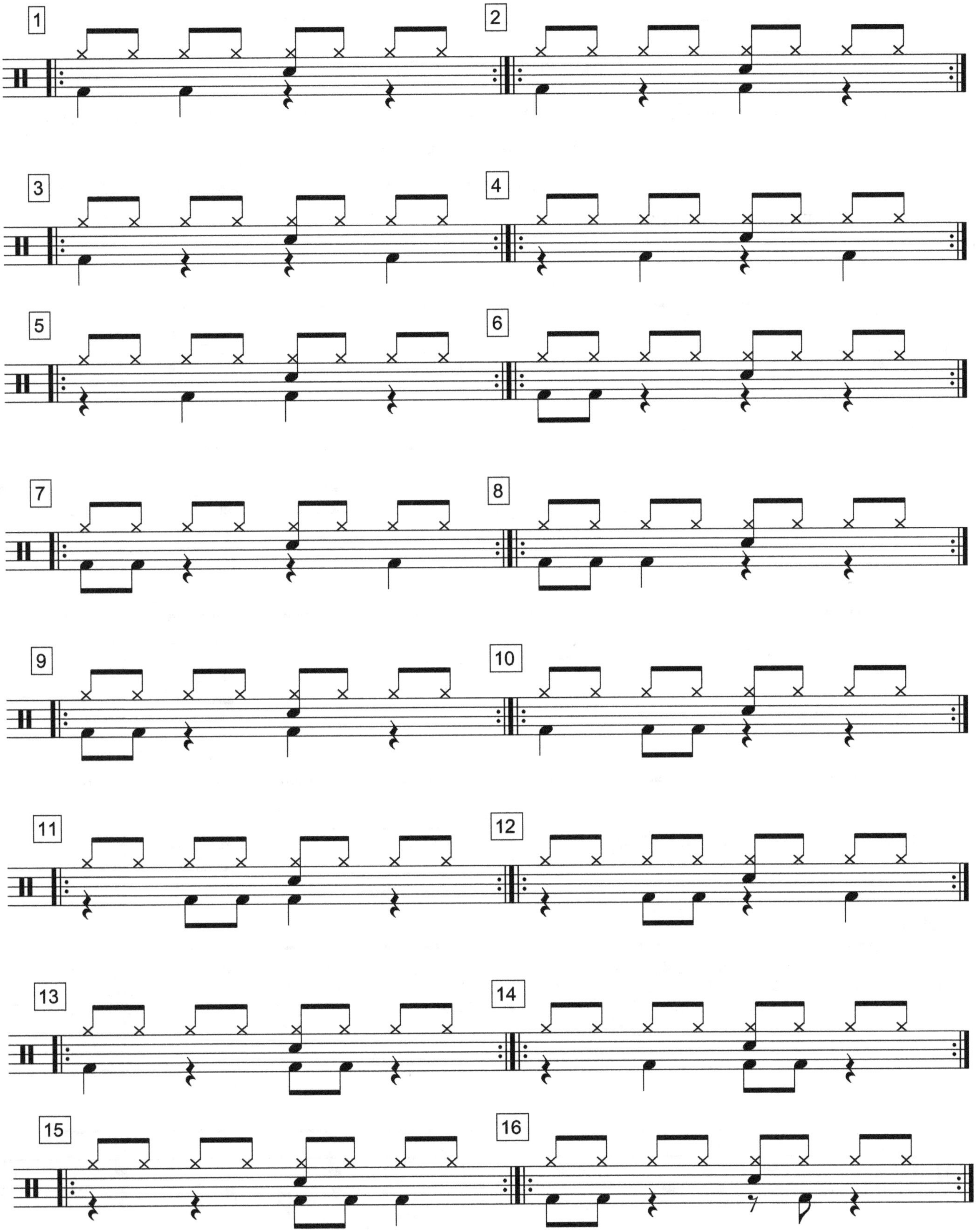

Remember the main focus is still the bass drum placement.

2 Bar 8ᵗʰ Note Grooves

Just like we did with the quarter note grooves and their variations, we are also going to combine the previous 8ᵗʰ note groove variations to form 2 bar grooves. Just as before, make sure you focus all the way through the examples. Here are some 2 bar grooves in both regular time feel and half time feel:

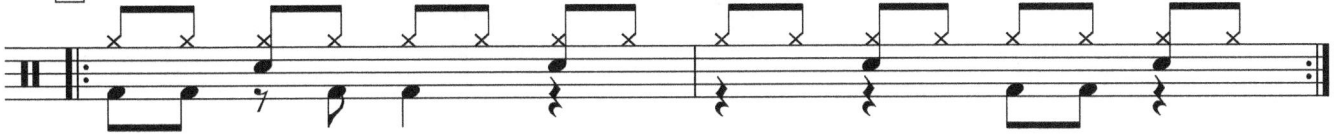

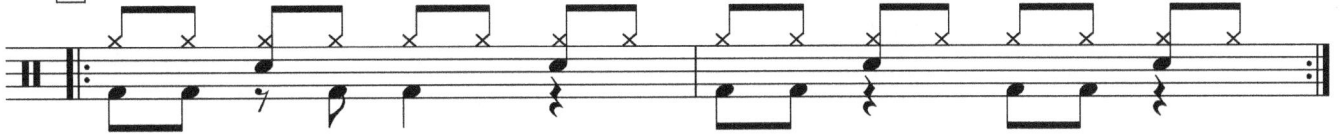

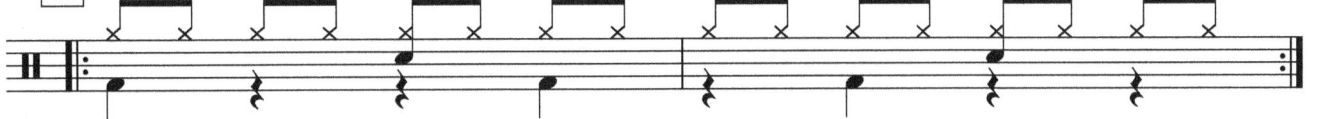

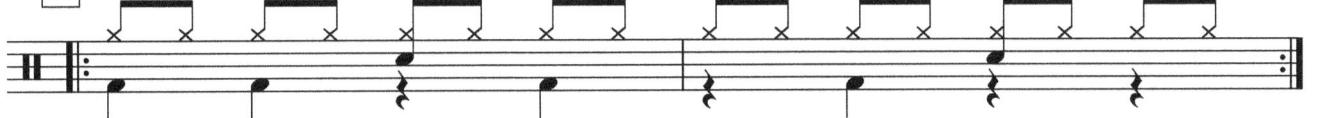

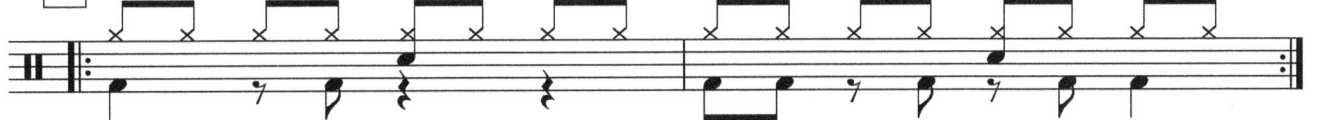

14

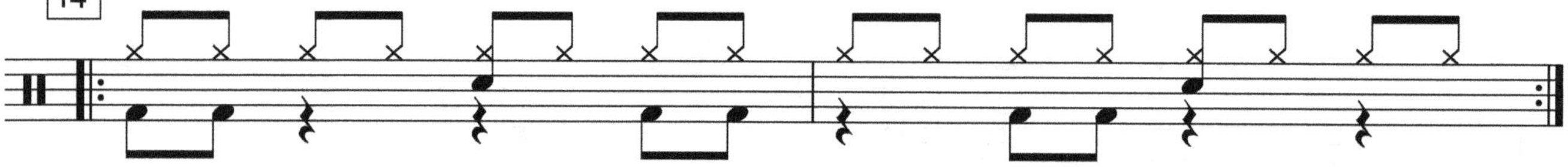

15

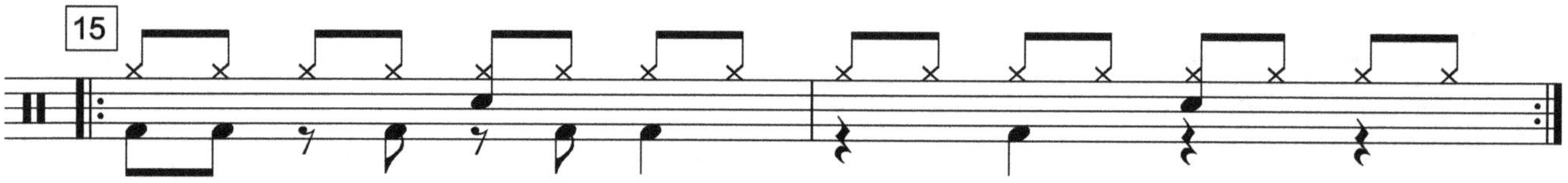

16

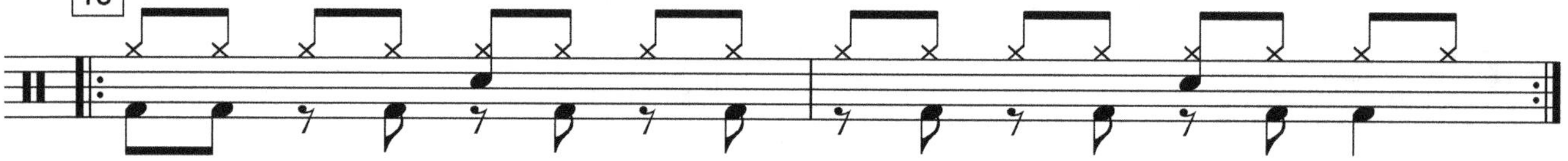

CHAPTER

Combining the Quarter Note and the Eighth Note

After playing a wide variety of both quarter note and 8th note grooves and spending some time working on reading quarter note and 8th note rhythms, it's time to put them together. In this chapter we will mix the two note values that we have studied so far, both in reading examples and behind the kit. We will start with a few reading examples.

Reading Example 3

There are a couple of ways of approaching the reading of combined note values. One is to always count the value of the note that you are about to play, and the other one is to always count the smallest subdivision on the example. Here's what I mean:

In example 1, we counted quarter notes when quarter notes are written and 8th notes when 8th notes are written. In example 2, we counted 8th notes all the way through, even though we didn't play 8th notes for the entire example. I'm going to encourage you to follow the counting system showed in example 2. The reason is, by always counting the smallest subdivision in the measure (in this case, the 8th note), we decrease the possibility of rushing the bigger note values (in this case, the quarter note). As drummers, respecting the correct note values is of utmost importance.

Here are several reading examples where we combine quarter notes and 8th notes. Remember to always count 8th notes:

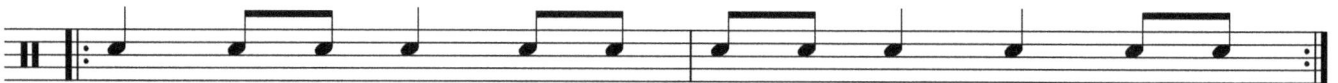

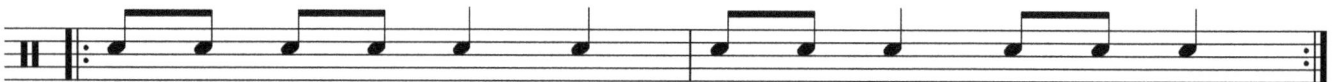

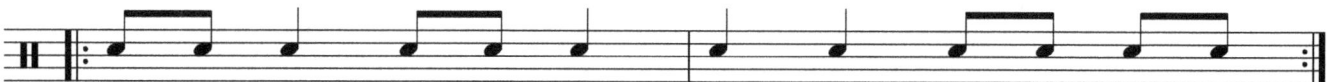

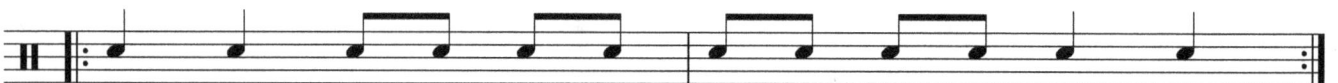

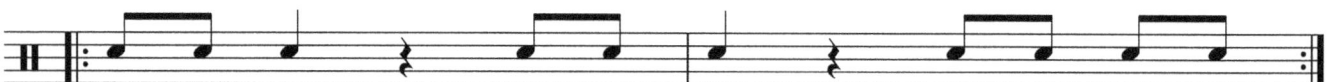

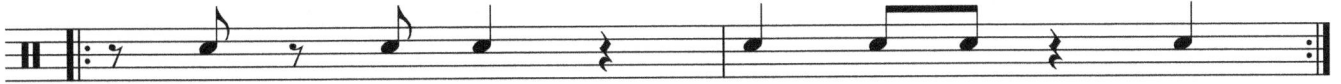

Your First Rudiment

When we talked about hand technique at the beginning of this book, we showed examples of how the hands are supposed to look over the snare drum or a "single surface". Practicing technique on a single surface (which could be a snare, a pillow, a practice pad, etc.) is vital for the development of our hands. Moving around the kit will always be more demanding than single surface; therefore, we must first develop control of our hands on a single surface.

In order to develop control of the sticks we use "rudiments". Outside of drumming, the word "rudiment" is often used to refer to a smaller section of a bigger concept. For drummers, rudiments are the foundation of our skills behind the kit. They are the technical exercises that we practice to develop the basic control over the sticks that we need to later move with freedom around the drum set.

The first rudiment we are going to learn is called the "single stroke roll". For the moment, we are going to use 8th notes to play it. When we play the single stroke roll we alternate between both of our hands and playing one single stroke with each, meaning that a stroke with the right hand will always be followed by a stroke with the left hand (and the other way around). Please note that below the 8th notes there are letters, those letters are called "percussion stickings" and refer to each one of our hands. "R" stands for right hand and "L" stands for left hand.

You might have noticed that even though it is one single rudiment, there are two ways to play it: right-hand lead (starting it with the right hand) and left-hand lead (starting it with the left). Normally for right-handed drummers right-hand lead will feel more natural, and for left-handed drummers left-hand lead will feel more natural. However we want to have control over both, so it is very important that we practice both the possibilities regardless of which one feels more comfortable. Ideally, we want develop a level of control where we don't have a preference for either one and feel comfortable leading with both hands. Make sure you practice the single stroke roll at different tempos and different dynamics for extended periods of time.

Fill Development

A big part of our job as drummers is to play fills. Fills are normally used as transitions, they are accents and rhythms that we play to mark the end of a section (for example, a verse) and the beginning of the next (for example, a chorus). We often play these transitions using several of the voices of our drum set. Unlike grooves, fills are supposed to stand out and usually break away from the groove to make a stronger transition. However, make sure you always respect the proper note values and that your dynamics are even between both hands.

In this section of the book, we explore several combinations of rhythms (quarter notes and 8th notes) and voices (different drums) to start developing our fill vocabulary.

To do this, we play three bars of groove and then a one bar fill. The groove that is written is the groove that we previously referred to as "2 and 4", however, you should try all these fills with any and all of the grooves that we learned previously in this book. In this first section of fill development, we use the "single stroke roll" that we learned earlier and move it around the kit. If you can't remember what each line/space in the staff means on your kit, go back to page 7 to refer to the drum key. We begin by playing a few fills using the single stroke roll as quarter notes; the main objective is to move around the kit:

1

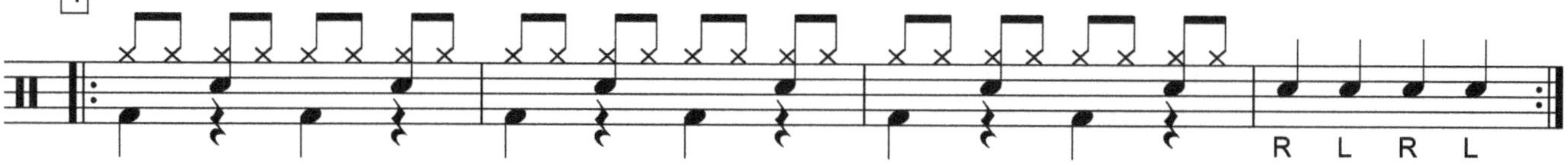

2

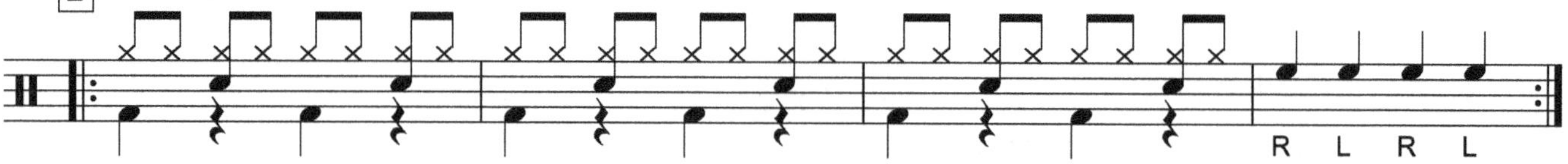

3

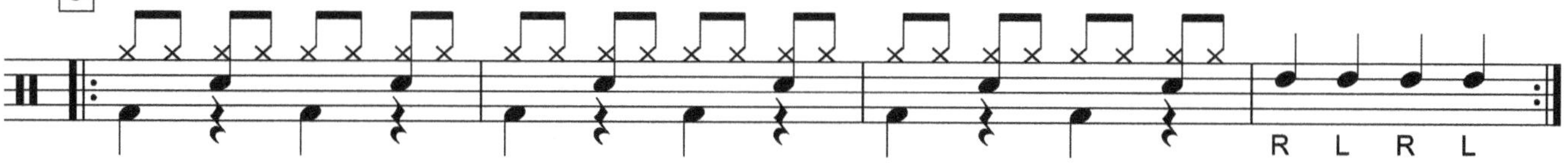

4

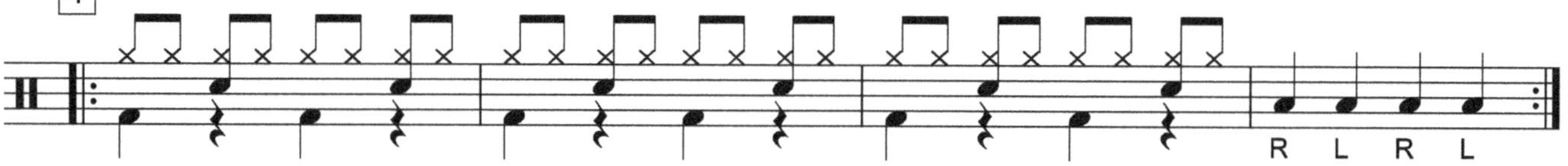

5

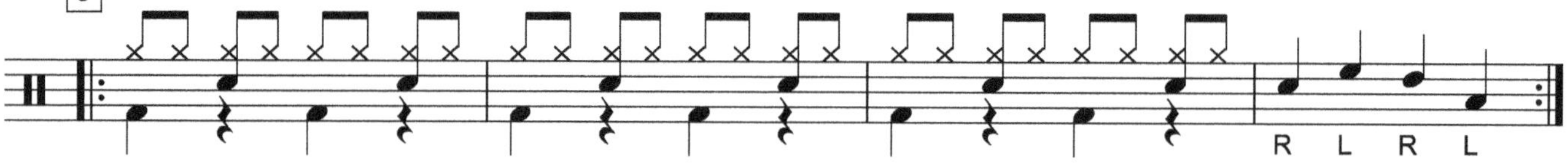

6

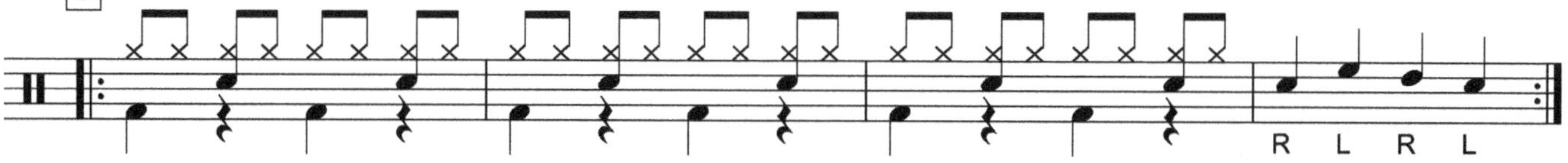

7

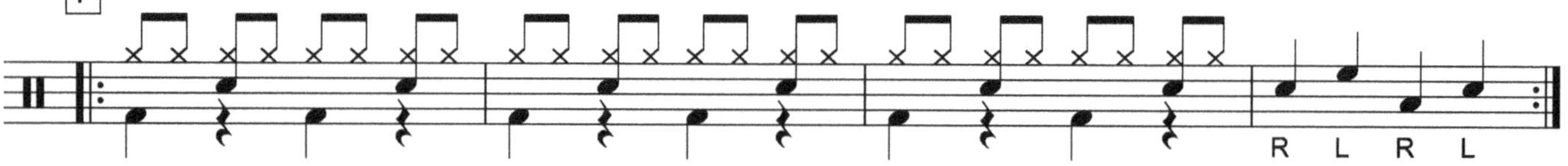

8

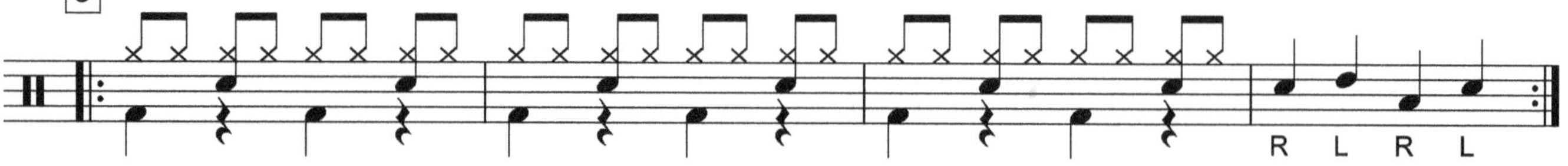

9

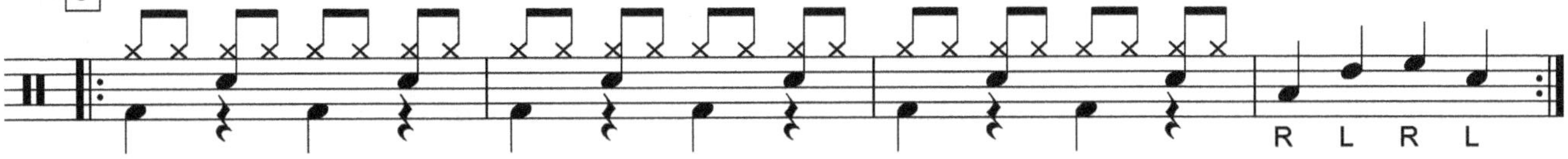

10

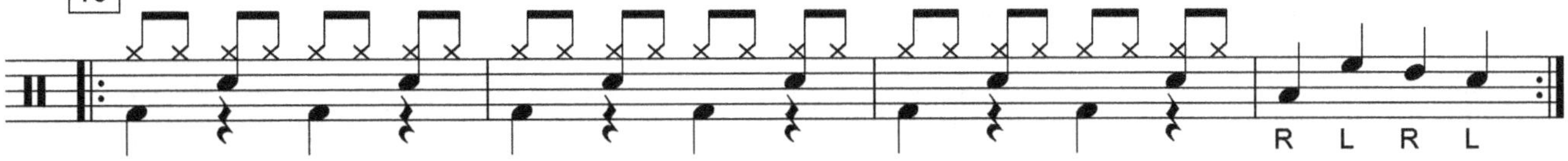

11

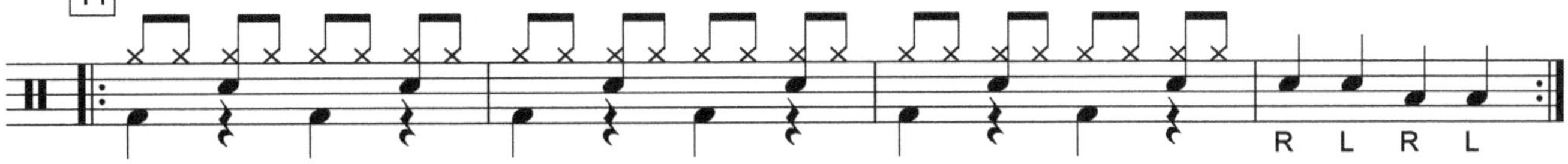

12

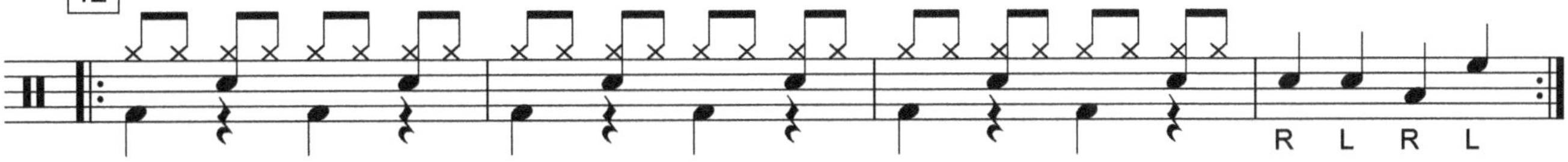

13

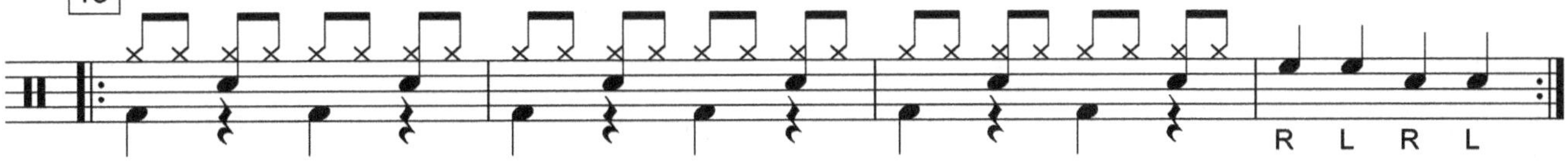

14

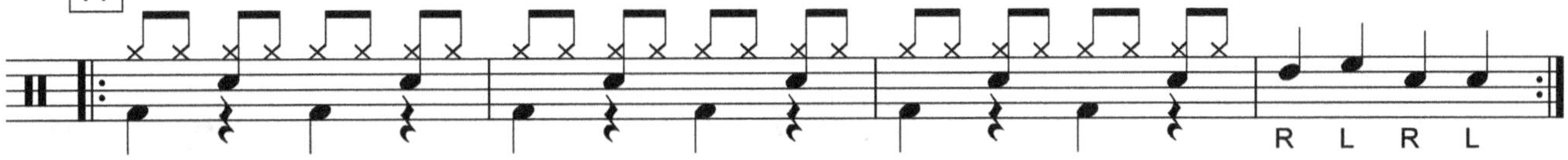

15

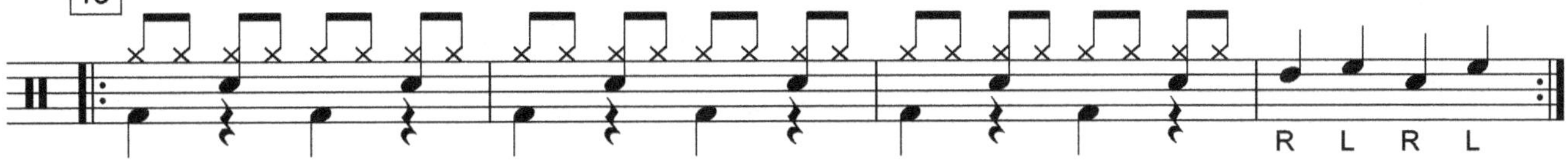

16

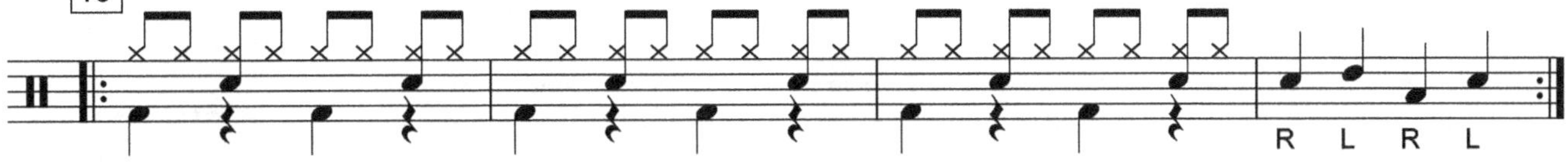

After moving around the kit for the first time with the single stroke roll and quarter notes, we are going to stick to the snare drum for a bit. The difference will now be in the rhythms. In the next few examples we combine quarter notes and 8th notes. Make sure that you count out loud:

8

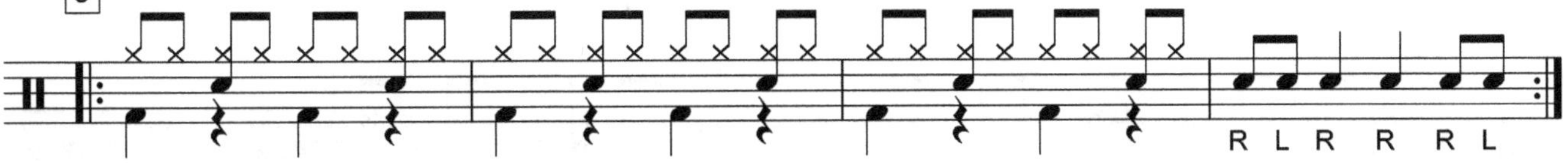

9

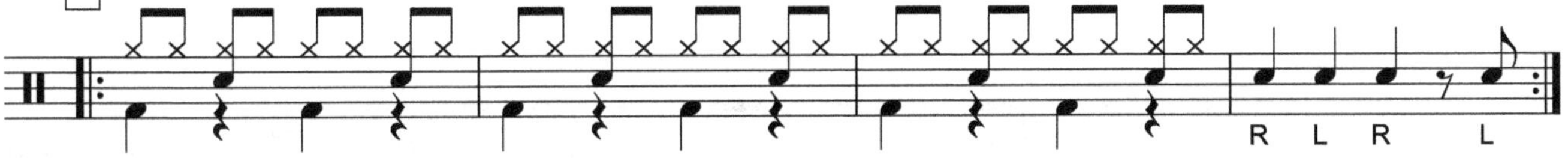

10

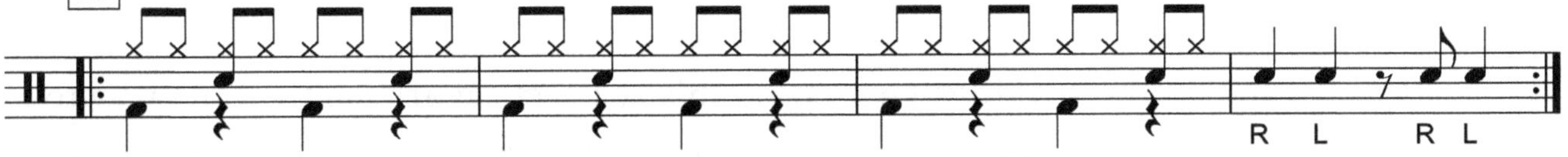

11

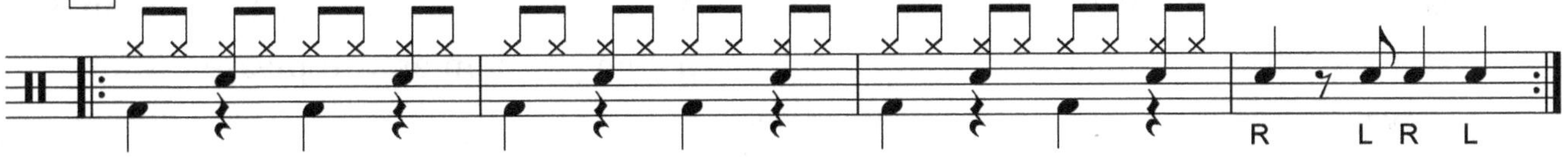

12

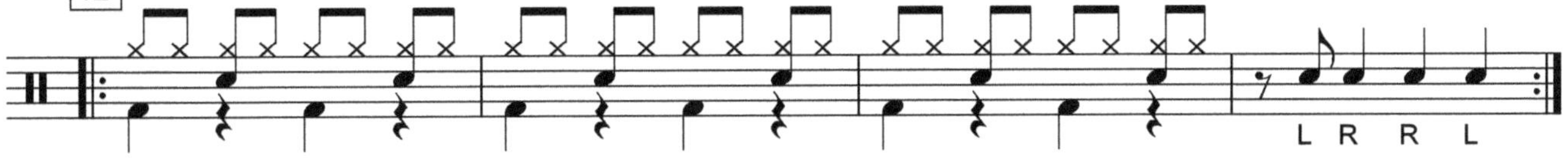

13

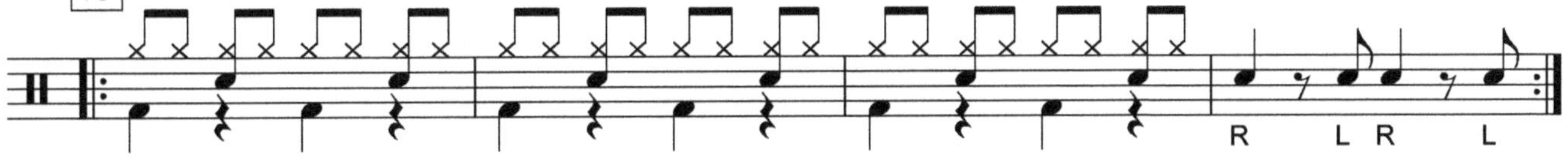

14

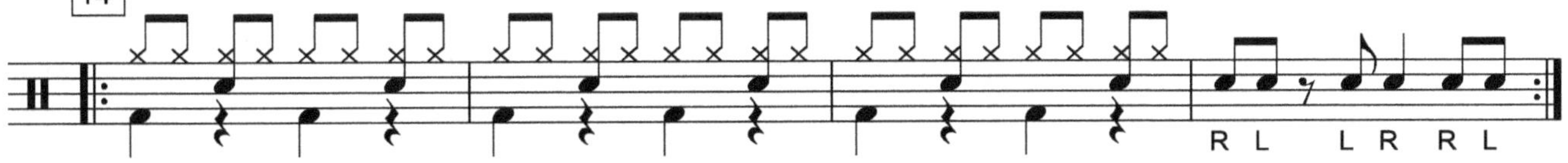

Please note that the stickings written on this last section are *not* the only way to play those fills. They are simply a suggestion based on my personal experience to make the playing of those rhythms easier. The reasoning behind those stickings lies in the fact that if we play the fills like that, we always have time to land on 1 (after the fill) with our right hand. Feel free to change them as you please if there's a way that helps you feel more comfortable.

After you get really comfortable playing all those fills on the snare and moving around the set playing quarter notes, it's time to develop them further. In this section, we repeat the fills that we played around the kit with quarter notes, but we play them all as steady 8th notes. This will be physically more demanding than the rest of the fills we have played thus far. The sticking that I recommend for the next set of examples is the single stroke roll. Make sure you count and that all of your 8th notes are even and have the same dynamics!

7

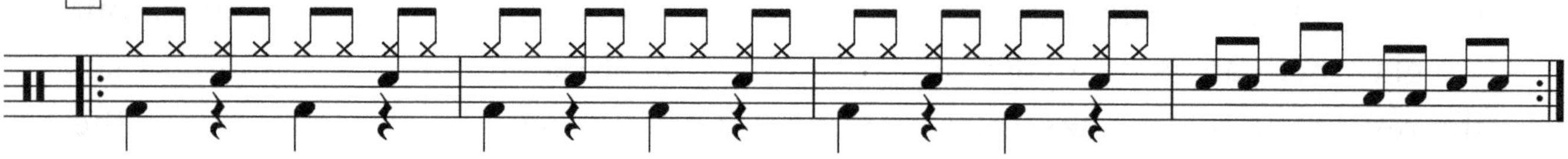

8

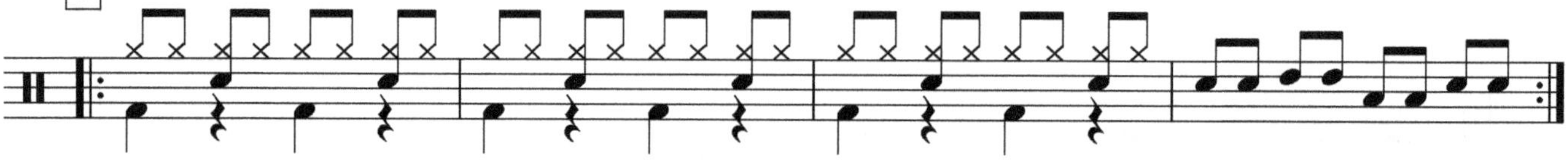

9

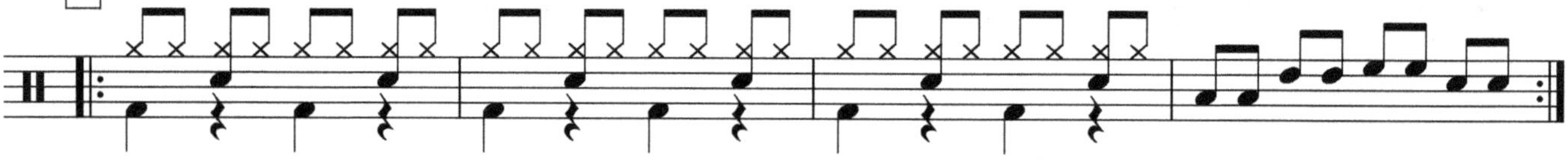

10

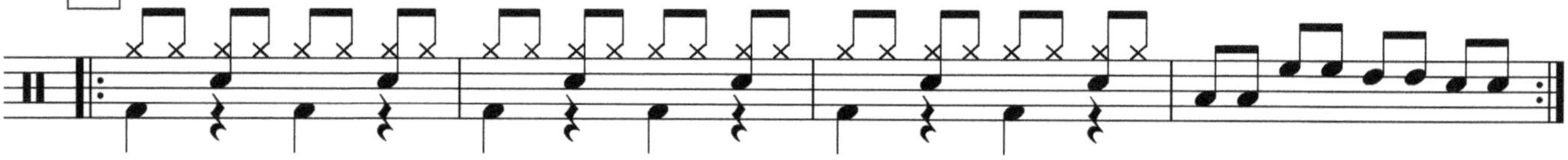

11

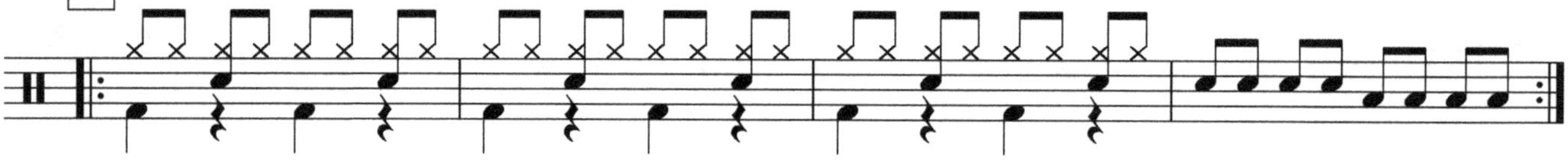

12

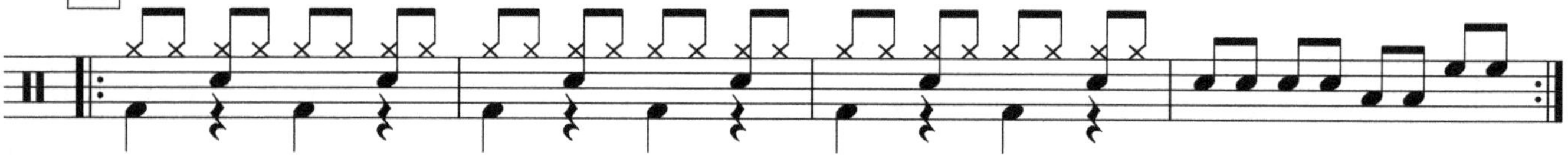

13

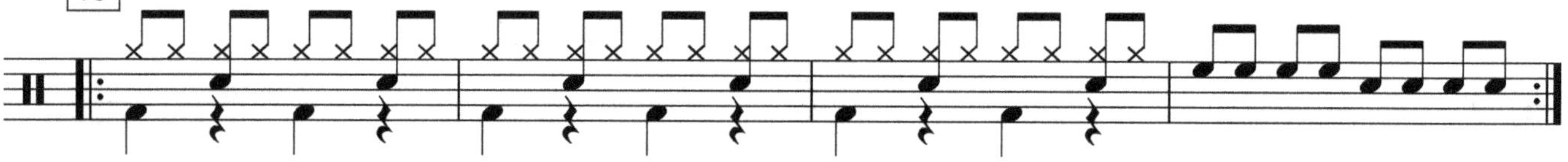

14

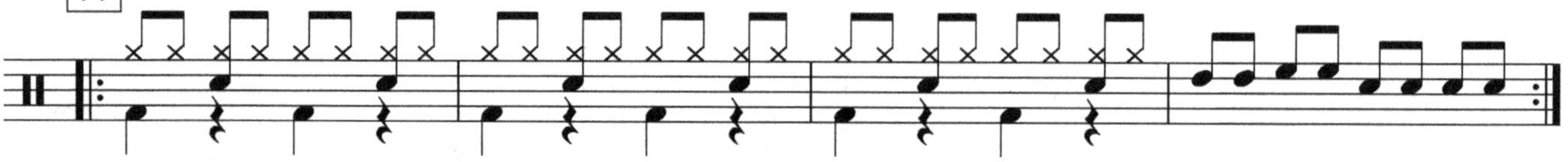

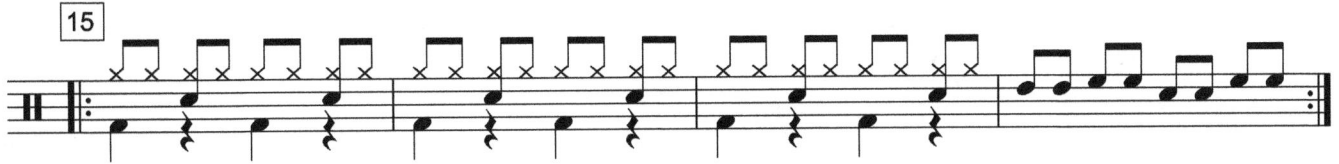

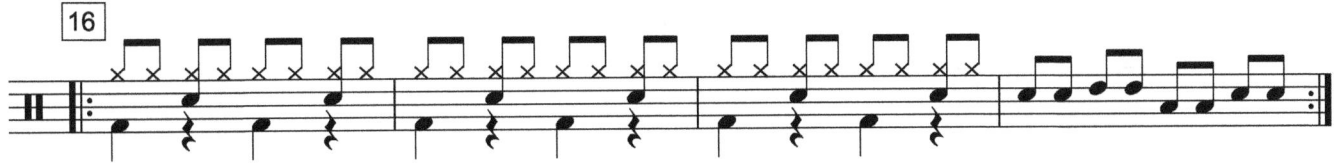

After you get comfortable moving those fills around the kit, there's only one thing left: to take the pre-established rhythms that we previously played only on the snare and change the voices as you please. Feel free to play whatever tom, snare, or cymbal you want, just make sure that you always respect the pre-established rhythm. This won't only force you to stay focused on playing the correct rhythm, but it will also be the first step towards improvisation. Have fun!

Chapter

6

New Note Values

Everything that we have learned so far has been based off of quarter notes and 8th notes. However there are many more rhythmic possibilities other than those two options. In this chapter, we learn a couple more note values. Both of which are bigger than the quarter note.

The Whole Note

We are going to start working backwards, exploring note values that are bigger than the quarter note. In chapter 1, we discussed the meaning of a time signature and how to figure out how many beats fit in one measure. We learned that 4/4 means that there are 4 quarter notes in one bar, and by now we also know that in a bar of 4/4 we can fit eight 8th notes (because each quarter note can be subdivided into two 8th notes, adding up to eight). But what happens if we want a note to be longer than a quarter note? What do we do if we want a note to last for the entire bar? That's when whole notes come in and this is what a whole note looks like:

Like the quarter note and 8th note, the whole note also has an equivalent rest that lasts for 4 beats. Here's what a whole note rest looks like:

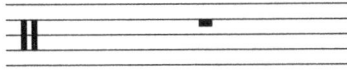

Reading Example 4

The whole note is worth 4 beats, meaning that it takes up the entire measure. Just as before, even if we have to play a whole note we still want to count all the beats out loud. This will help us avoid speeding up and slowing down as we hold a whole note and will help us give the note its full value. Something that is very important to know is that as drummers we are unable to hold notes. Every single drum on the kit has a very short sound. The only instruments in our kit that can ring for a long time are cymbals. When we hit a drum, we have no real or controllable sustain and because of that, it is even more important that you count out loud. If we played a melodic instrument, say piano or trumpet, we would be able to hold notes and give the whole note its full value. Please ask your teacher to demonstrate the difference between a whole note played on a practice pad or a snare drum and a whole note played on a keyboard or guitar. This will help you have a better understanding of what "holding a note" really means.

Now let's go through some reading examples that combine whole notes and quarter notes. Because quarter notes are going to be our smallest value please make sure you count quarter notes out loud and give all the notes their full value:

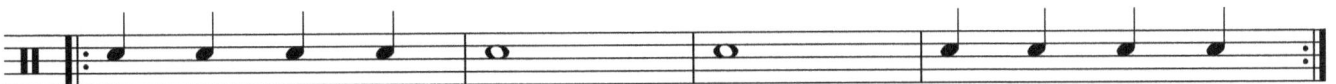

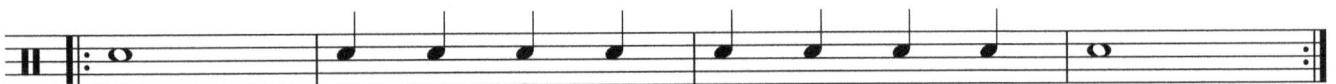

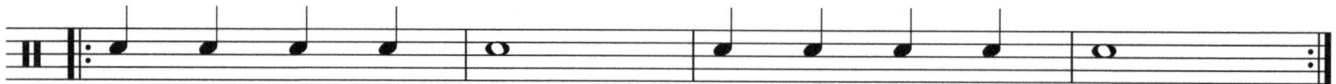

3

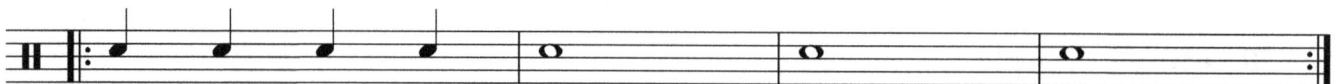

4

The Half Note

We now know a note value that is worth one beat (the quarter note), a note value that is worth four beats (the whole note), and a note value that is worth half a beat (the 8th note). Now we are going to learn a note value that is worth two beats. This note is called a "half note" and it looks like this:

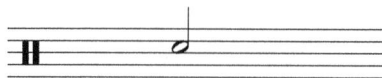

Like all the other note values it has an equivalent note rest that looks like this:

Reading Example 5

Because the half note is worth two beats, a time signature of 4/4 would require us to have two half notes to complete the bar. Just like with the whole note, please ask your teacher to play you the difference between a quarter note and a half note on an instrument that can hold notes to help you understand the difference even more. Now, let's go through some reading examples that combine half notes and quarter notes. Remember to count all the beats out loud and to give all the notes their full value:

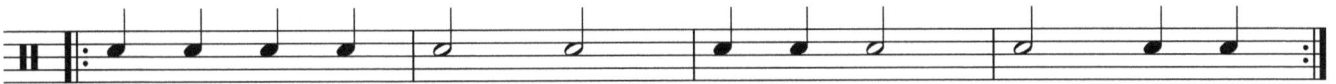

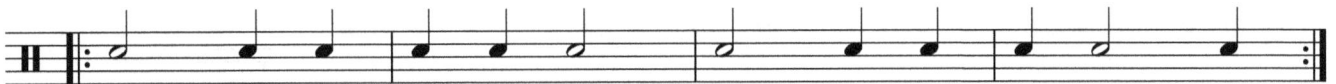

Reading Mixed Note Values

In this section, we go through some more reading examples, but now we are going to combine all the note values that we know. This means that we might have whole notes, half notes, quarter notes, and 8th notes all in the same example. Because 8th notes are the smallest note value that we know, please make sure you count 8th notes out loud throughout all the examples.

Reading Example 6

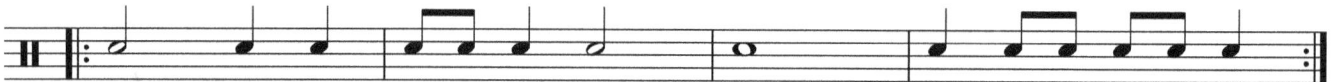

8

9

10

CHAPTER

7

The 16th Note

In the previous chapter, we learned the half note and the whole note, both with values bigger than the quarter note. The 16th note is a smaller value than the quarter note; in fact, it is the smallest note value that we have learned yet. The 16th note, 16th note grooves, and 16th note fills are all extremely common in today's contemporary music. That's why it is essential for us as drummers to really understand this subdivision and get comfortable playing 16th notes.

Let's find out where the 16th note comes from. Earlier in this book we said that an 8th note is the result of evenly subdividing the quarter note into two and that the counting system is "1 and, 2 and..." and so on. The 16th note is the result of evenly subdividing the quarter note into four. This means that in the same space where we used to play one note (the quarter note), we will now play four evenly subdivided notes. Just as with the 8th notes, we want to acknowledge all of the 16th notes when we count, so we add two more syllables to our counting system. We keep the same numbers as before on the downbeats and the "and" for the upbeats, but now we will add the letter "e" and the letter "a" to the two new notes. These two notes (the two 16th notes that are not the downbeat or the upbeat) are referred to as the "off beats". This is what one bar of 16th notes in 4/4 looks like:

| 1 | e | + | a | 2 | e | + | a | 3 | e | + | a | 4 | e | + | a |

The 16th note also has an equivalent rest. Here's what a single 16th note rest looks like:

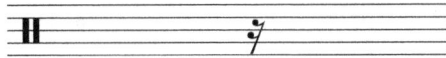

Another way to think about where the 16th note comes from is to think "down the pyramid" of note values that we know so far. The biggest note value that we know is the whole note, if we split that into two we get the half note, if the split that into two we get the quarter note, if we split that into two we get the 8th note, and now if we split the 8th note into two we get the 16th note. Here's a graphic description of this rhythmic pyramid that will help you better understand how all the note values relate to each other:

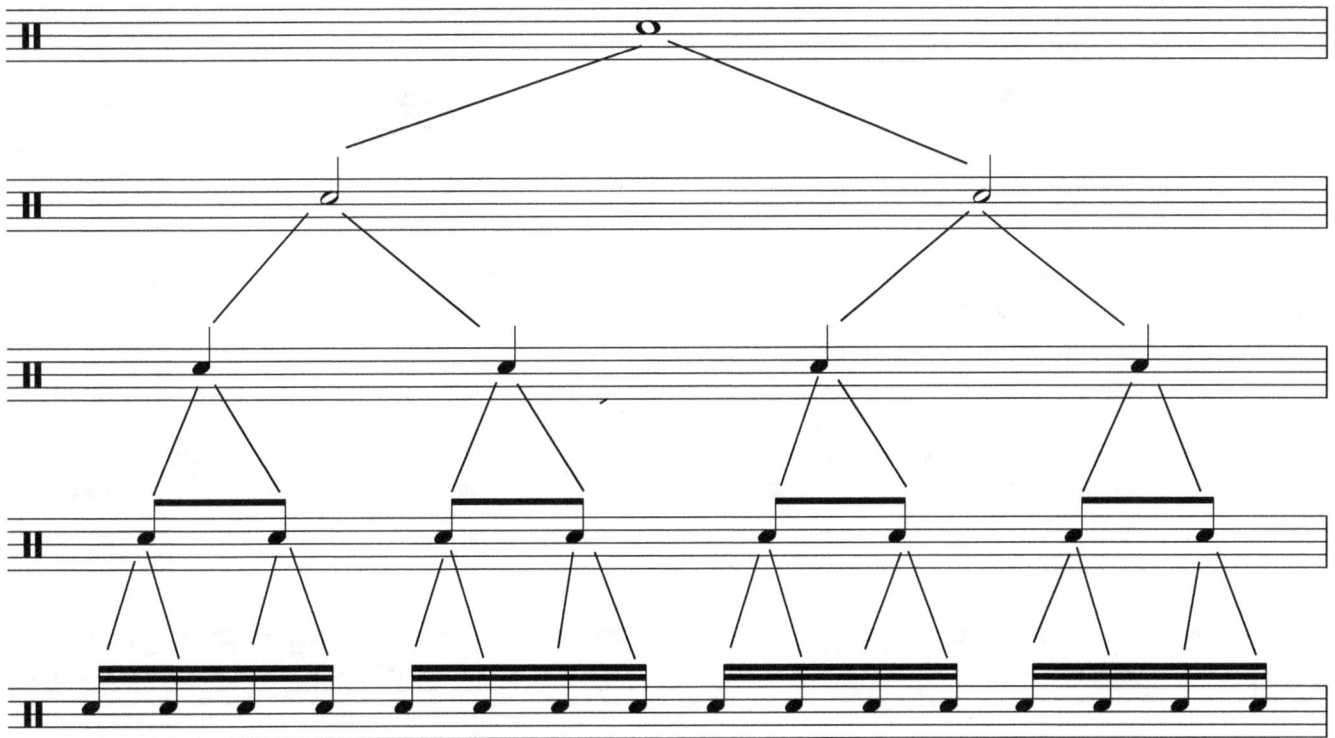

Reading Example 7

We now combine quarter notes, 8th notes, and 16th notes in some reading examples so we start getting used to the relationship between them. Because the smallest note value that we are playing is 16th notes, please count 16th notes all the time to help us keep better time, and to make sure we give all the notes their full value:

9

10

Your First 16th Note Grooves

Now that you are a bit more familiar with how we count 16th notes and how they relate to the other note values we've studied, it's time to put the theory into practice behind the kit. Just like in Chapter 4, the first step to playing 16th notes on the kit is to focus on bass drum placement. However, this time our hi-hat hand is playing steady 16th notes instead of steady 8th notes. The bass drum (for now) plays only 8th note figures and nothing on the off beats. In fact, we repeat the grooves from Chapter 4, as far as bass drum placement, but we keep 16th notes on the hi-hat. Please note that it is all right if you have to slow the grooves down to be able to play steady and even 16th notes with your hi-hat hand. It is much better to play the examples slowly and accurately, rather than too quickly and inaccurately. Here's what the first bass drum examples we studied look like with 16th notes on the hi-hat:

9

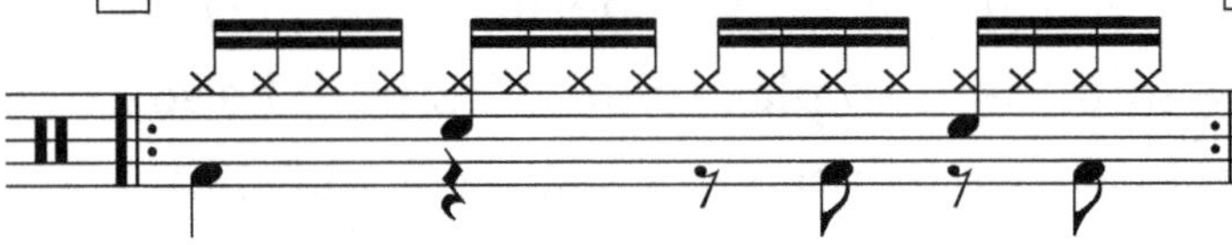

10

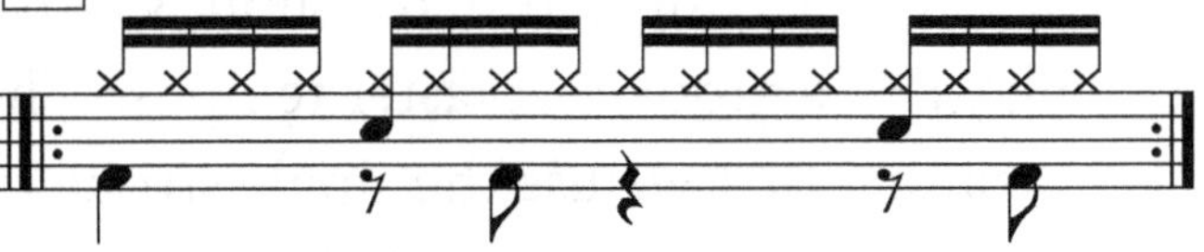

11

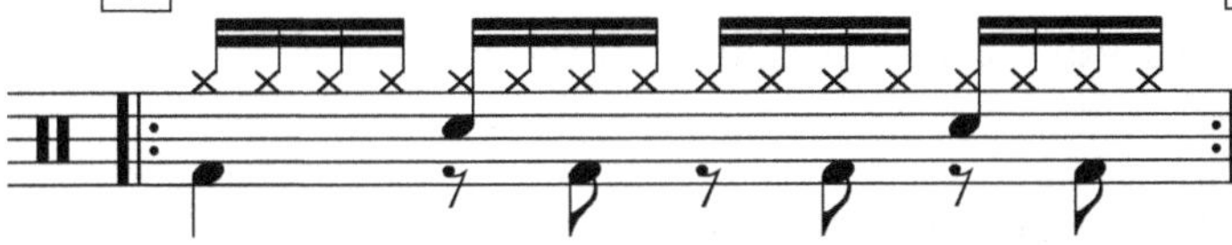

12

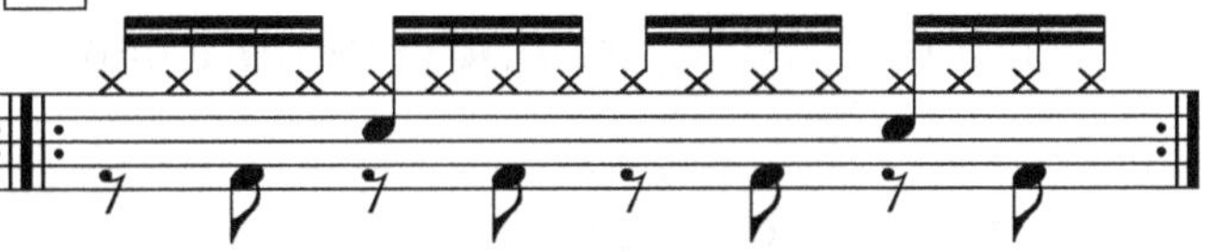

13

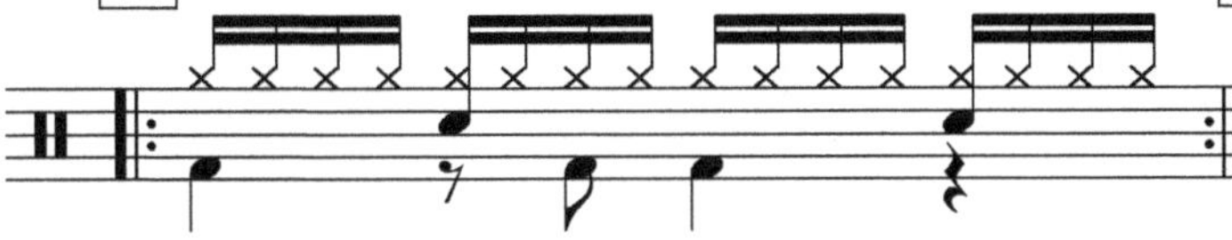

14

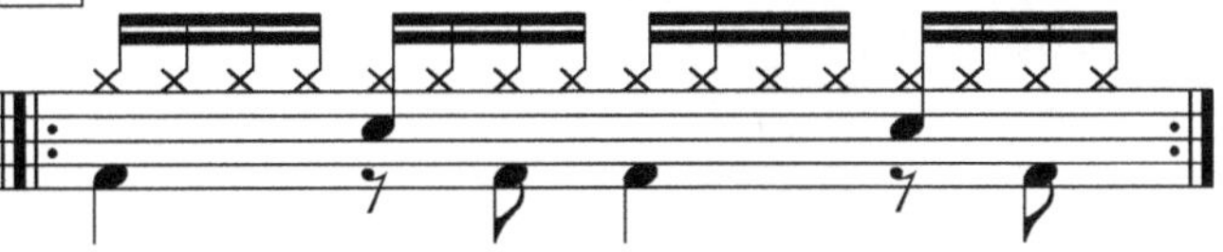

15

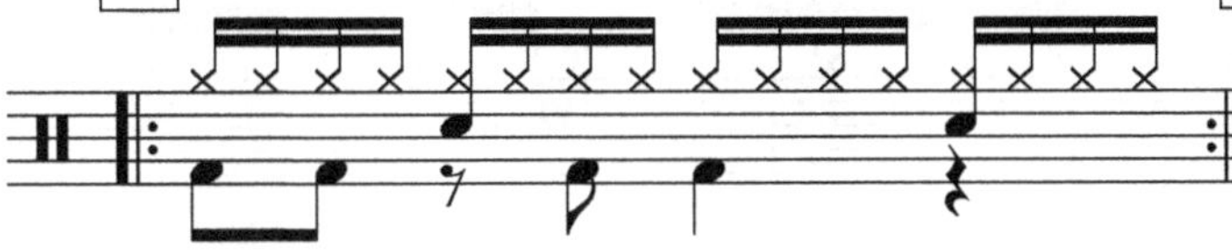

16

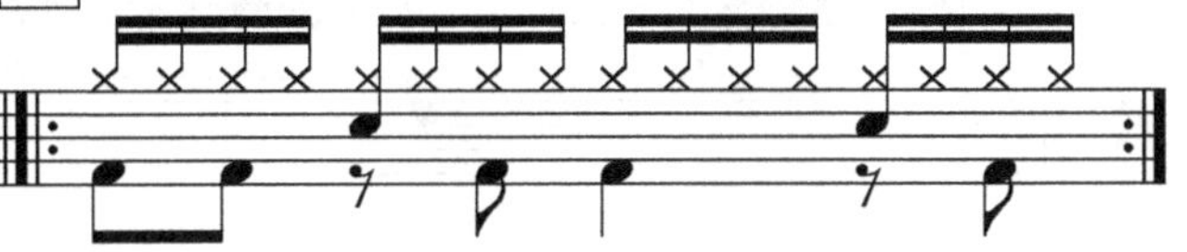

17

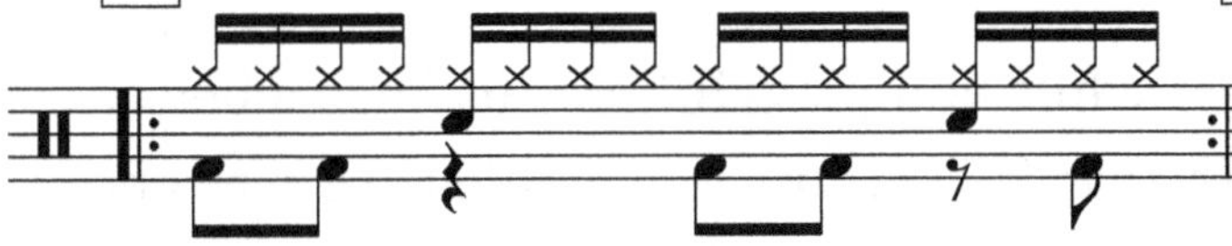

18

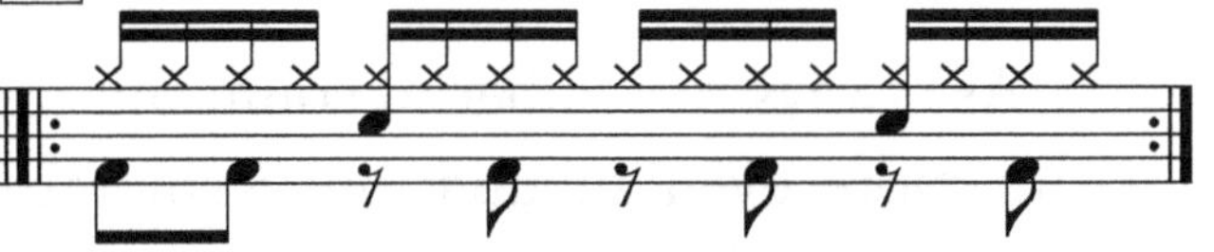

19

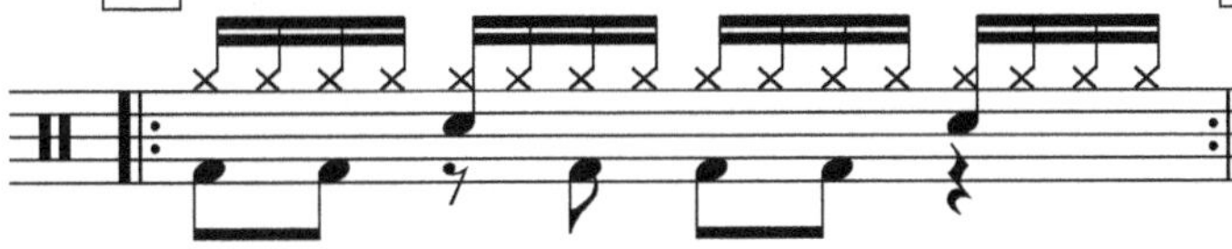

20

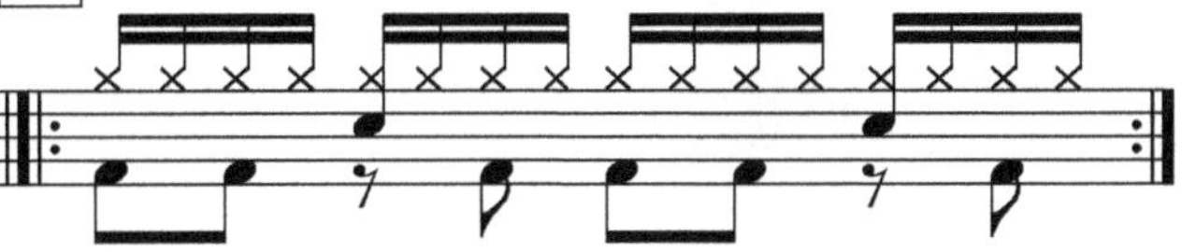

Two Handed 16th Note Grooves

After playing those 16th note grooves, you might be wondering how can we play those grooves at faster tempos? The solution is to play them with both hands, meaning that we use the single stroke roll that we learned in Chapter 5 and split it between the hi-hat and the snare drum. Just as before, we want to keep the "back beat" (snare) on the downbeats of 2 and 4. As a result, we have to miss a 16th note from the hi-hat on those beats. Because the snare is a much more dominant sound than the hi-hat, it's not very noticeable and very common for us to do this.

Before getting into the grooves, let's figure out the hands. Note that the sticking of this next example matches the sticking of the single stroke roll we learned in chapter 5:

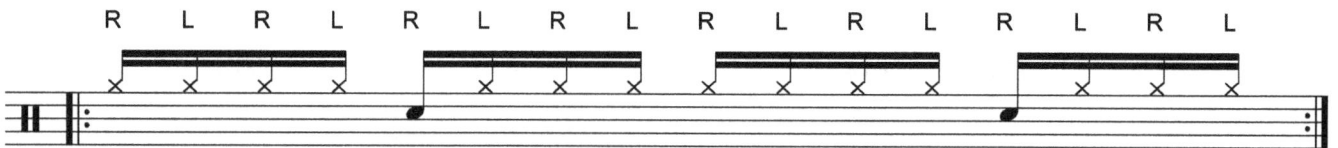

As always remember to count out loud while you play. It helps us keep a better and more even subdivision. Remember that if you are left-handed, you might want to start this pattern with the left hand instead of the right.

Once you are comfortable with the hand pattern, it's time to once again focus on the bass drum placement. In this next set of examples, we repeat the previous grooves, but play the two handed groove on the hi-hat. Pay special attention to how (if you are right handed) all of the bass drum strokes line up with the right hand and make sure that your bass drum is always playing with your hi-hat in unison. The sticking is there only for the first 3 examples but it should be kept the same for all of the examples:

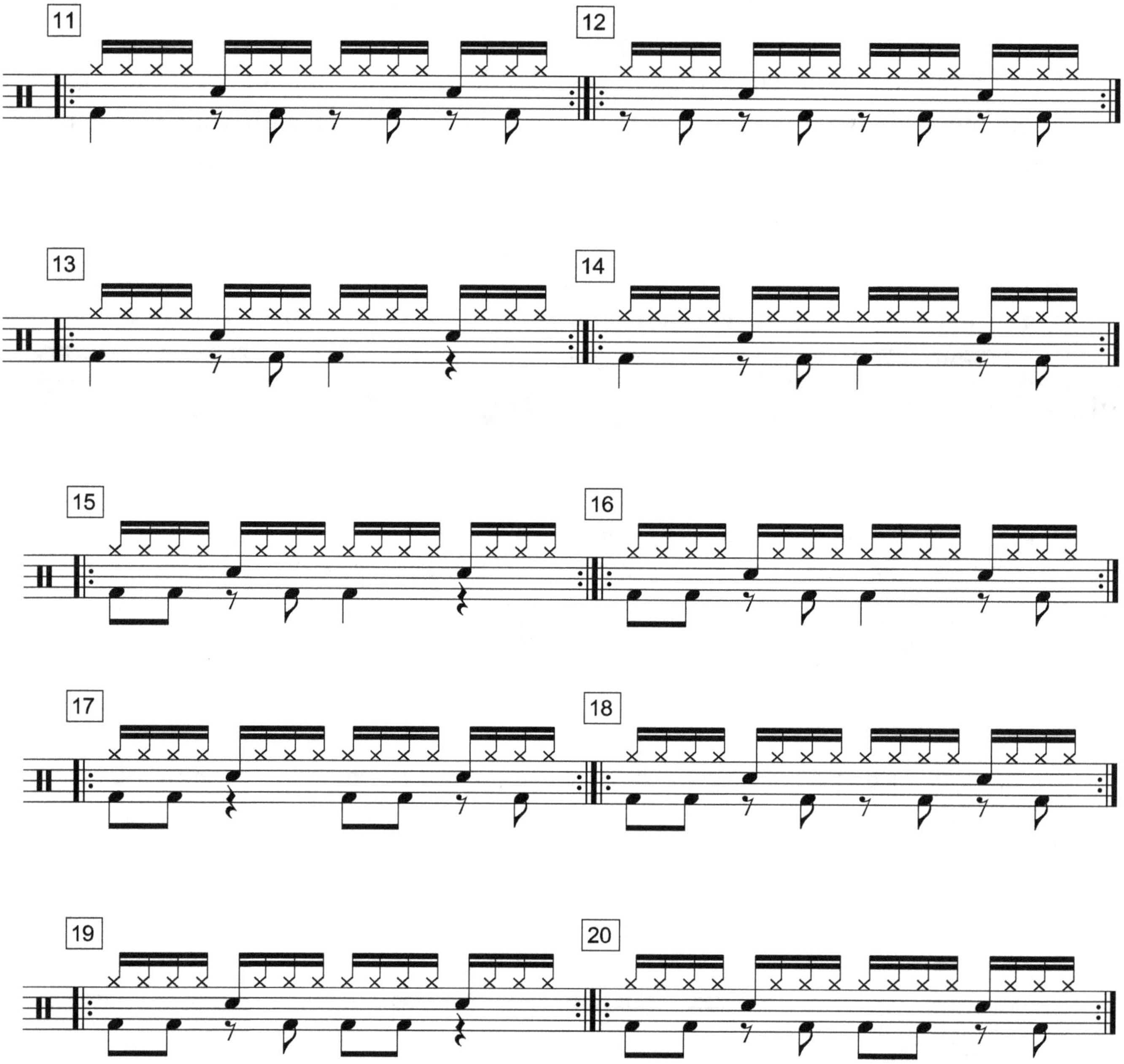
11
12
13
14
15
16
17
18
19
20

CHAPTER

16th Note Bass Drum Placement

Before we can start developing 16th note bass drum placement, we need to learn a new notation called "dotted notes". This is a subject that will come up often in the future and is very useful for us as drummers because it simplifies the reading and writing of complex rhythms. Please read the next section of this chapter very carefully and make sure you understand the meaning of "dotted notes".

Dotted Notes

A "dot" adds half of a note's original value. For example, if you have a quarter note with a dot to the right of it, the note is worth three 8th notes. The reason for that is that half of a quarter note is a single 8th note, so by adding an 8th note to a quarter note (which is equivalent to two 8th notes) you end up with a note that is worth three 8th notes. It looks like this:

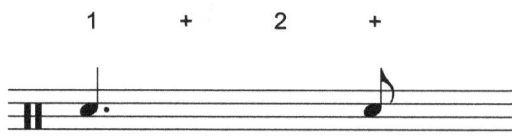

The reason why there's an 8th note after the dotted quarter note is that I wanted to keep the example as two full beats. Again, because the dotted quarter note is worth three 8th notes in order to complete the second beat I had to add that last 8th note.

If we were to complete a bar of 4/4 with a dotted quarter note followed by an 8th note it would look like this:

In both examples, please pay attention to the counting on top to make sure you understand it correctly and make sure that you are playing lines up with what is on the page.

The same concept applies to any and all note values. If you have a half note (which is worth 2 beats) with a dot next to it, it is worth 3 beats (because half of 2 beats is one, and that's what we are adding to the note because of the dot). If you have a dot next to a whole note (which is worth 4 beats), it is worth 6 beats (because half of 4 is 2).

More importantly for us, this concept applies to the 8th note as well. We learned in the previous chapter that if you split one 8th note into two you get two 16th notes, which means that half of an 8th note is one single 16th note. So, if we see an 8th note that has a dot next to it, its real value is three 16th notes (again, because we are adding half of its original value to it). If you see a dotted 8th note on the downbeat, you need to add a 16th note rest after it to complete the beat, which looks like this:

You can also reverse that figure and have the 16th note rest on the downbeat followed by a dotted 8th note. This means the dotted 8th note lands on the "e" and because it's worth three 16th notes, it completes the beat. That figure looks like this:

Here are two bars of a dotted 8th note on the "e" with repeat signs. Play it a few times in a row counting out loud to make sure you understand where it lands and how the dot affects the 8th note:

Off Beat Bass Drum Placement

Up to this point in the book our bass drum has been limited to only playing downbeats and upbeats, which means that our hi-hat and our bass drum have always lined up. However, we can also play the off beats (the "e" or the "a") with the bass drum, which tends to be a little more challenging because for the first time our bass drum and our hi-hat hand will not line up (if we are playing 8th notes on the hi-hat). Because of that it's going to be particularly important for us to count out loud to make sure that we are placing the bass drum on the correct 16th note.

We are going to start exploring this one 16th note at a time, first only playing bass drum and hi-hat. Let's play the first 16th note of the beat on the bass drum while keeping steady 8th notes with the hi-hat hand, which looks like this:

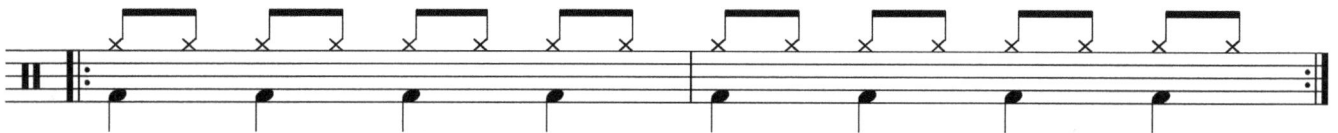

Note that because this is a downbeat, the bass drum lines up with your hi-hat.

Now we will play the second 16th note (the "e") with the bass drum while keeping 8th notes on the hi-hat. This is the first time that your bass drum won't line up with the hi-hat. Instead, it lands in between the two hi-hat strokes:

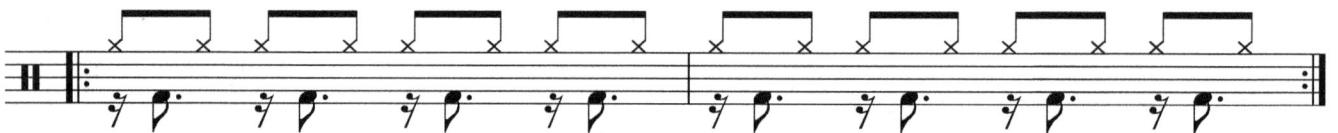

Following the same order, it is now time to play the bass drum on the third 16th note, which is the upbeat. We have done this before, but for the purpose of this set of examples, please review it:

Last is the "a", the last 16th note of the beat. Just like the "e", it will not line up with the hi-hat, so make sure that you are counting out loud and that your bass drum lines up with your counting:

The point of these examples is to learn how to place the bass drum in all of the four possible 16th notes of every beat. In order to feel how the 16th note is being displaced by one 16th note every time we switch examples, we are now going to play all four examples in a row. We will play two bars of each example and without stopping we are going to move on to the next one. This means we play two bars of the downbeat, two bars of the "e", two bars of the "and", and two bars of the "a". Here's what that looks like:

Make sure to count out loud so that you don't lose the "1", meaning that you want to make sure you always know where the downbeats (especially beat 1) are even if you are moving the bass drum around. Drummers knowing where to find the 1 is of crucial importance, so don't forget to count!

Adding the Snare Drum

Now that we have put some work into the mechanics of playing the bass drum in all of the possible 16th notes that there are in a beat, it is time to start incorporating that into grooves. We start by playing 8th notes with the hi-hat hand and 2 and 4 with the snare while repeating the previous set of examples:

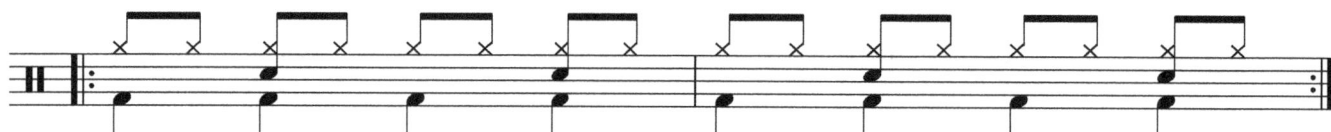

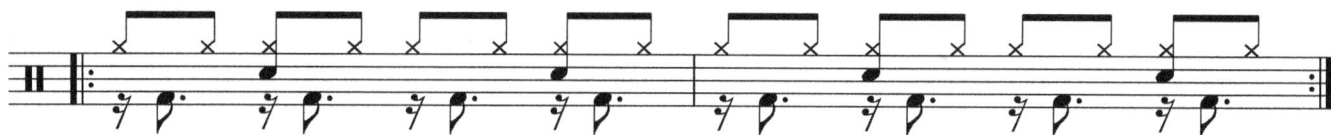

Just as before, we play all four of them without stopping, but this time the snare will also be involved, always playing on beats 2 and 4. This is what it looks like:

As always, don't forget to count out loud.

Grooving with the Off Beats

After getting used to incorporating the snare drum, it is time to start changing the bass drum patterns to create new grooves. Please note that the examples below develop 16th note by 16th note, meaning that at the beginning of the examples we'll be playing a lot of "e's", then a lot of "a's", and at the end we combine them. As always, remember to count out loud and start as slowly as necessary, remembering that speed is an outcome of control and not the other way around.

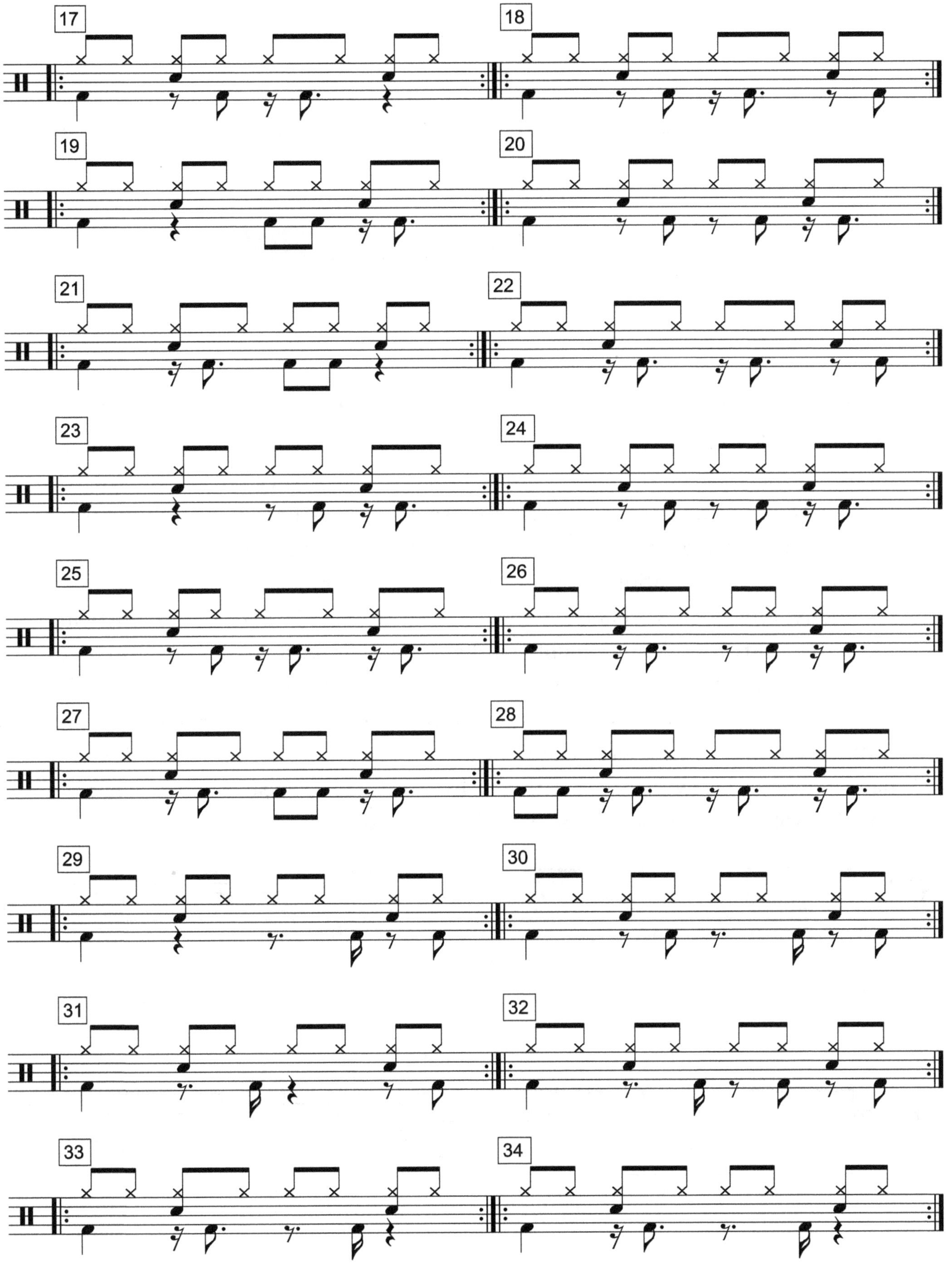
17
18
19
20
21
22
23
24
25
26
27
28
29
30
31
32
33
34

CHAPTER

9

The Double Stroke Roll

In chapter 5, we learned our first rudiment, the "single stroke roll" [1]. In the last chapter of this book, we are going to learn another basic rudiment called the "double stroke roll". Just like the single stroke roll, it is very important that you start working on this new rudiment on a single surface first. It doesn't matter if you use a pillow, a practice pad, or the snare drum as long as while you do it you are paying extra attention to your technique. If you have any doubts about technique, refer back to chapter 2 and ask your teacher. When we are practicing technique exercises, like the double stroke, it's very important that we also focus on the rhythm, meaning that we want to make sure we give the notes their full value and that everything is dynamically even. The double stroke roll is played by hitting two strokes with each hand, meaning we play two strokes with the right hand followed by two strokes with the left hand, and repeat. Here is what the double stroke roll looks like when played as 8th notes:

R   R   L   L   R   R   L   L

L   L   R   R   L   L   R   R

_____

[1] Page 51.

Just like the single stroke roll, the double stroke roll can be played starting with the right or the left hand. Note that above it is written both ways. Make sure that you practice both variations and remember to count out loud.

At this stage of the book, your knowledge of rhythm and note values is much broader than it was when we learned the single stroke roll and we are going to use that to our advantage to help us develop the double stroke roll. We are going to switch note values every two bars but we are going to keep the sticking for the double stroke roll intact throughout the entire example. Because the smallest subdivision that we play is 16th notes (the smallest subdivision we have studied so far), make sure that you count 16th notes throughout the entire example. This helps you keep a steady tempo and give all the notes their full value. Also make sure that you consider how fast the 16th notes are going to be and make sure you can play the double stroke roll at that tempo before you start playing the example. Since that is the smallest subdivision, it will be the most challenging one to play. Here's what the example looks like:

When you are practicing the previous example, make sure to pay attention to the subdivision, the dynamics, and the tempo. We want all of those things to be nice and steady!

Combining Rudiments

Before we apply the double stroke roll to the drum set, we are going to combine the two rudiments that we have learned so far. This is really effective for developing our hand technique because switching between the two rudiments requires more hand control than repeating the same one over and over again, even if we change the subdivision while we do it. It also improves our ability to focus because it requires that we concentrate more to make sure we change rudiments at the right time. The first thing we are going to do is play two bars of each rudiment as 8th notes. Because of the nature of the exercise, it is very easy to add accents that are not written and it is very important to make sure that all the notes are even dynamically and rhythmically.

As always, make sure you count out loud.

We are now going to expand upon the exercise and add changing note values to it. As always, make sure your dynamics are even, that you count out loud, and that you focus for the entire duration of the example. I also encourage you to repeat it several times to exercise your focusing skills. Here's what switching note values and alternating the single and double stroke roll looks like:

Changing Note Values for the Double Stroke Roll

At this point, we have switched note values and rudiments in the same example, but we haven't switched note values while switching rudiments. This means that every time we've played the single stroke roll with quarter notes, it has been followed by the double stroke roll also with quarter notes. In the following example, we are going to play one note value for the single stroke roll followed by the double stroke roll with a different subdivision. This is a really fun and practical way to practice the development of the double stroke roll because often when we play the double stroke roll we also double the subdivision (for example, we go from 8th notes to 16th notes). In this first example, we switch between quarter notes and 8th notes:

R L R L R L R L R R L L R R L L R R L L R R L L

This second example is very similar, mechanically it's exactly the same as the previous one, but the counting system changes. Make sure that you count 16th notes all the way through the example:

R L R L R L R L R L R L R L R L R R L L R R L L R R L L R R L L R R L L R R L L R R L L R R L L

The next example includes 16th notes as well. We are going to play one bar of the single stroke roll with quarter notes, followed by one bar of the double stroke roll with 8th notes, return to the single stroke roll with quarter notes, and then play the double stroke roll with 16th notes at the end. Feel free to repeat the example many times until you get comfortable with the changes. Here's what the example looks like:

R L R L R R L L R R L L R L R L R R L L R R L L R R L L R R L L

Begin practicing this example as slowly as necessary to maintain a steady tempo. Gradually increase the *speed without letting it get out of control.

Musical Examples

Here are a few musical examples you can use as a reference for some of the grooves that we played in this book. Most of the grooves we learned are used in pop and rock music, so most of the bands/artists in the examples below play those genres of music. I encourage you to relate all of the examples in this book to live and recorded music. After all, we learn how to play the drums to play music, not to practice on our own. Have fun and listen to the grooves in the next few examples.

The "2 and 4" groove, see page 37 :
Billie Jean, by Michael Jackson
The Reason, by Hoobastank
Whiskey in the Jar, by Metallica

Example 2, see page 38:
Living After Midnight, by Judas Priest

Example 4, see page 38
Smells Like Teen Spirit, by Nirvana (verse)

Example 13, see page 39 :
Because of You, by Kelly Clarkson

Example 6, see page 42:
Pretty Fly, by The Offspring (verse)

Example 1, see page 71 :
The Hand That Feeds, by Nine Inch Nails

Level 1 Test

If you've made it this far into Level 1 of this series, you have learned some of the most basic, and yet most important aspects of drumming. You have a clear understanding of quarter notes, 8th notes, and 16th notes, as well as the single and double stroke roll. Before we can move on to the next level of this series we need to take a quick test. More than a test, I want you to think of it as a short review of everything you learned in this level.

If there's anything in this test that you can't play, or don't understand, please find the section in this level that develops that concept and review it. Don't move on to Level 2 until you can comfortably play everything in this review test. You have already played all of the examples in this review, if they are not exactly the same, they are very similar to some of the examples in this level, therefore, you should be able to understand them and play them.

The examples on this test are numbered and follow a similar developing order as everything in this book; however, they are no longer methodically built from easier to harder. For the first 3 examples, please write (or tell your teacher) the name of the items that the arrows are pointing at. Other than those 3 examples, everything else is playing and shouldn't need an explanation.

1

2
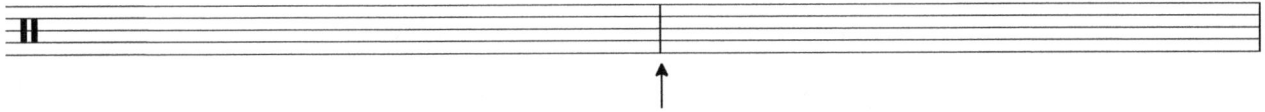

3
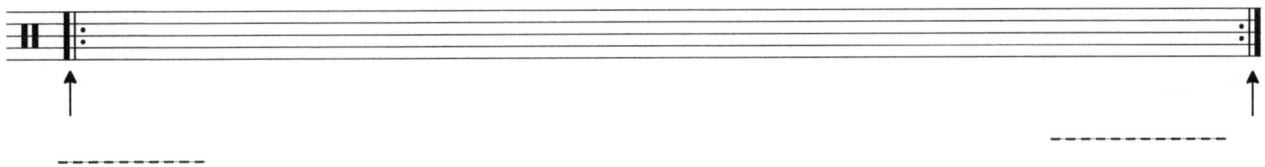

4

5
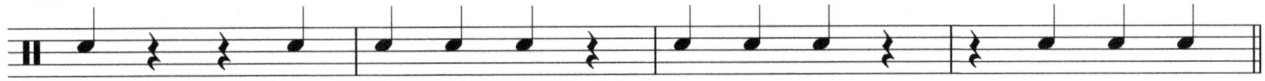

6

7

8
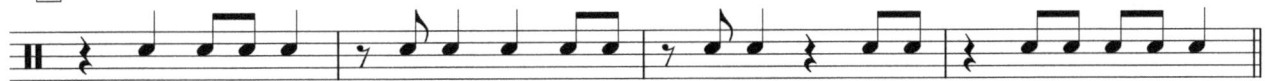

9   **10**

11
12
13
14
15
16
17
18
19
20
21
R L R L R L R L R L R L R L R L
R R L L R R L L R R L L R R L L

Level 1 Review

In this book, we've learned some of the most basic, yet most essential concepts for drumming. Even if you have successfully played everything in this book, it does not mean you are finished with it. Perhaps the most exciting thing about playing drums is that there is always, and I mean always, room for growth. I encourage you to return to this book once you have completed Level 2 of this series and review all of the examples here. Once your skill set is higher, you will discover new things from this book that you may have originally missed. A higher level of understanding and technical skill provides opportunity for more advanced application of these fundamental concepts. Becoming a better drummer is a never-ending process and I hope you have enjoyed the beginning part of your process. Let's go on to Level 2!

ABOUT THE AUTHOR

Ray Rojo first tried playing his neighbor's drum set at age 13 and has been "hitting stuff" ever since. Originally from Mexico, he studied privately with Abundio Lopez before joining Yamaha School of Music. He then continued his studies at a music college in Mexico City called "Academia de Música Fermatta" until 2009 when he changed colleges and countries to attend Musicians Institute in Hollywood, California. At Musicians Institute, he studied privately with Jeff Bowders and completed his Bachelor of Music degree in Performance of Contemporary Music.

While at Musicians Institute, he joined a metal band called Fractalline with whom he toured India and the United States. While in India, Ray also worked as a clinician in several cities for Furtados Music Stores. Ray has also toured the United States and Europe with 14-string guitar player Felix Martin and his trio. He joined progressive metal band Polarization and toured with them as well. Ray also performs as a session player and recorded drums for the book Advanced Rhythmic Concepts fro Guitar by Jan Rivera. His developing career led him to become a Tama drums artist in December of 2012.

In addition to his career as a performing artist, Ray currently teaches at Modern Music School in Pasadena, California where he has over 20 drum students. He also works at Musicians Institute as a Teacher's Assistant. He has also been a Private Tutor whose responsibilities include helping students with drum performance and technique, chart-writing, and music theory.